ALLAH IS LIGHT

ALLAH IS VISIBLE

KHAL SALEM (ALKARKARI)

Published by Hemingway Publishers

Cover design by Hemingway Publishers

ISBN: Printed in the United States

In the name of Allah, the Merciful, the Compassionate.

May Allah strengthen our connection with our master Muhammad and his family, as He did with our master Ibrahim and his family. May Allah bless our master Muhammad and his family as He has blessed our master Ibrahim and his family.

After the initial edition of "Allah is Light. Allah is visible" was released, I was thrilled by the encouraging feedback. To enhance the text, I invited readers to provide suggestions, which prompted me to revise by dividing the long chapters and incorporating illustrative figures to clarify the concepts.

I express my gratitude to Sidi Sheikh Muhammad Fauzi Alkarkari (May Allah Sanctify His Secret) for his spiritual guidance, education, and oversight. He deserves full credit for the guidance provided, while I acknowledge any shortcomings or instances of unclear authorship.

I want to express my gratitude to all the readers who shared feedback, as well as to my children, Meryam, Zak, and Essie, and their mother, Beki, for their support and encouragement.

I want to thank my godchildren, Emma (Ouiam) and Abdellah, for being incredibly supportive sounding boards for my ideas.

I want to express my gratitude to the developers of the Quran.com website, which I frequently consult for their Quranic translations available on the free public interface. May Allah greatly reward them for their good deeds.

Finally, I want to extend my heartfelt thanks to the members of the publishing team at Hemingway Publishers—Nathan, Ana, and Jason—for their unwavering support throughout my publishing journey.

The Institute of Nur Karakri Institute (INK) Author Association

This book is the inaugural publication from the Nur Karkari Institute (INK) Author Associates, founded by the author. The INK Author Associates

The mission is to engage a diverse group of writers who can inspire others to embrace the ideals of:

1- Brotherhoods
2- No compulsion.
3- Complementation.

INK author association aims to attract individuals from diverse belief systems to participate in the meaningful practice of tolerance, acceptance, and dialogue among people of faith who are eager to begin their internal journey of self-discovery

INK Author Associates Purpose is:

- Writing as a legacy
- Encourage robust dialogue
- Leave marks long after we pass

Khal Salem (Alkarkari)

Table of Content

Chapter 1
"The Revelation of Lordship and Servanthood"

Allah loves to be known, though no one exists alongside Him.

This profound statement highlights the paradox of existence—how can our existence be both real and illusory? Is intelligence truly the right tool to comprehend Allah? Allah's love for being known sets into motion a creative process, leaving traces behind. Creation, then, becomes an illusory byproduct of divine love. It is like casting a stone into a still pond: while the ripples are visible and tangible, the water itself remains undisturbed. Similarly, while creation appears genuine, it reflects Allah's presence alone.

This principle extends to sound, which emerges when energy moves through air. For instance, as air flows through a flute, it produces sound. Our minds often misinterpret what we can name as definitive reality; however, these "named" things are part of an illusory cascade of existence referred to as "other-than-God."

"I cherished being recognized. I crafted my creation to ensure they would know me through me" (Divine Quote).

'Allah has been, and nothing exists alongside Him. ' (Hadeeth)

The Level of Lordship (Rubūbiyya)

The concept of Lordship represents the relationship between the educator and the educated. It seeks to convey the profound prophecy, or tremendous news (al-naba' al-ʿaẓīm), of the divine Essence, names, and attributes. However, Lordship itself does not explain Divinity (ulūhiyya); rather, it creates a relational system where meanings (maʿānī) ascend and descend. These meanings are first understood by the primary Intellect or the Muḥammadian Reality and then by dispersed, lesser intellects among the believers. This system reveals what Allah loves, commands, and wishes to disclose.

The tangible, auditory, and visual illusions surrounding us—such as shapes, figures, planets, and material forms—are described in the Qurʾān as the "worlds of knowledge" (al-ʿālamīn) of the Lord. This vast universal structure, encompassing the seven heavens and seven earths, is akin to a multilevel library governed by a single librarian who plans, replenishes, provides information, and sustains both the library and all within it.

Servanthood

On the continuum of being blinded by proximity and cursed by distance, there is an optimal starting point for servants on their learning path. Closeness to the educator can lead to a decrease in the student's knowledge. Conversely, the further a student is from the educator, the greater their ignorance and the lesser their understanding. Therefore, the ideal starting point for education is represented in a temporal-spatial model of personalized learning, as illustrated in the narrative of Adam's descent to Earth. Adam's Earth represents the ideal state, with Adam symbolizing personalized conscious awareness. In contrast, Satan embodies ignorance, denying the possibility of awareness or understanding.

Allah is both manifested and unmanifested. To help His creation grasp the concept of being veiled and unveiled, He created the illusion of time, marked by the cycles of day and night and the changes in our

2

physical composition. This also includes the spatial illusion concerning the limited capabilities of our external senses.

Various limitations constrain human perception: our vision is restricted to specific color frequencies, our hands have maximum lengths and capabilities, and our feet can only travel so far. Hypothetically, we could argue that Adam's descent involved adding layers that obscured his boundless internal senses. As a result, he had to rely on external senses to navigate his way back during his journey through these barriers in the material world, a challenge that also extends to his descendants.

Two ways to reconnect with the original reality beyond time and space and explore a more profound truth are through death or mystical wayfaring. After death, one's vision sharpens, external senses fade, and internal senses take precedence. In contrast, during mystical wayfaring, under the guidance of an authentic sheikh, one can experience an unveiling while still alive on Earth. The wanderer may glimpse how to see, feel, and move in alignment with the divine secrets entrusted to them from the beginning—possibly even before the creation of time and space—allowing them to taste the essence of divinity.

The wayfaring experience suggests that the Lordship elevates the servant's awareness toward Divinity. However, as previously mentioned, the concept of Lordship gnosis does not fully explain Divinity (ulūhiyya). Instead, it illustrates a system of transcendence where meanings (ma'ānī) ascend and descend, understood by a primary intellect and several smaller, dispersed mini-intellects. This system facilitates the revelation of what Allah desires, commands, and wishes to disclose.

3

Guidance for Lordship During the Stages of Humankind's Devolution

How did humankind evolve through the temporal-spatial construct? And what is the role of the Lordship? Moreover, what is Lordship?

The relationship between an educator and the educated exemplifies the concept of Lordship (rubūbiyya). Its purpose is to convey a great prophecy or significant news (*naba' 'aẓīm*) about the divine essence, names, and attributes.

The tangible, auditory, and visual illusions, such as shapes, figures, planets, and embodied constructs, are called the worlds of knowledge. This vast universal structure of seven heavens and seven earths is likened to a multilevel library under the sovereignty of one librarian who plans, replenishes, supplies information, and sustains the library and its inhabitants.

Humankind had a holy-like phase that preceded its being as "things." Allah tells us that humankind's reality or origin is very secretive, pure, and so subtle that it is impossible to describe or mention. *Has there come upon the human being a period when he was nothing to be mentioned?* (Q Insān 1)

Creation is the Outcome of Reenacting the Divine Command 'Be':

The creation process involves several steps: Allah desired to be known, issued a command (*Al-Amr*), articulated a statement (*Al-Qawl*) to define the boundaries of disclosure, and created an illusionary existence perceived through non-existing traces. Like a rope, these traces shape the effects of the divine command. This can be likened to a light source in a movie theatre, creating multidimensional moving objects. If the electrons are removed, the characters disappear.

The critical difference is that human characters were granted intellect, vision, hearing, and the ability to name things. This led them to misidentify others and believe they owned the secret of existence.

Despite differences in characters, shapes, images, layers of veiling, depth of mental dominance, and permissible differentiation, these three facets of disclosure share a similar reality. Their purpose, outcome, and the moral of the story about the great prophecy of Allah revealing Himself are alike.

This book delves into the Lordship Slogan, "Praise to Allah, the Lord of the worlds," which is the second verse of the first chapter of the Quran. As seekers progress, the next slogan would be for the Deity: "There is no God but Allah." The transition between the two slogans is "in the name of Allah, the Merciful, the Compassionate."

Lastly, the universe continuously praises God by enacting His will or reenacting Allah's command. This reenactment is eloquently described in the Quran as the "validation of the divine word," where the divine word represents the command meant to be disclosed (be). Allah said: *"Those are the ones upon whom the word has come into effect, among nations which had passed on before them of jinn and men"* (Q Ahqaf 18)

The divine flow transcendence:

Allah's revelation of Himself occurs in a descended manner by adding veils to transition from the absolute ineffable reality to the metaphorical one.

5

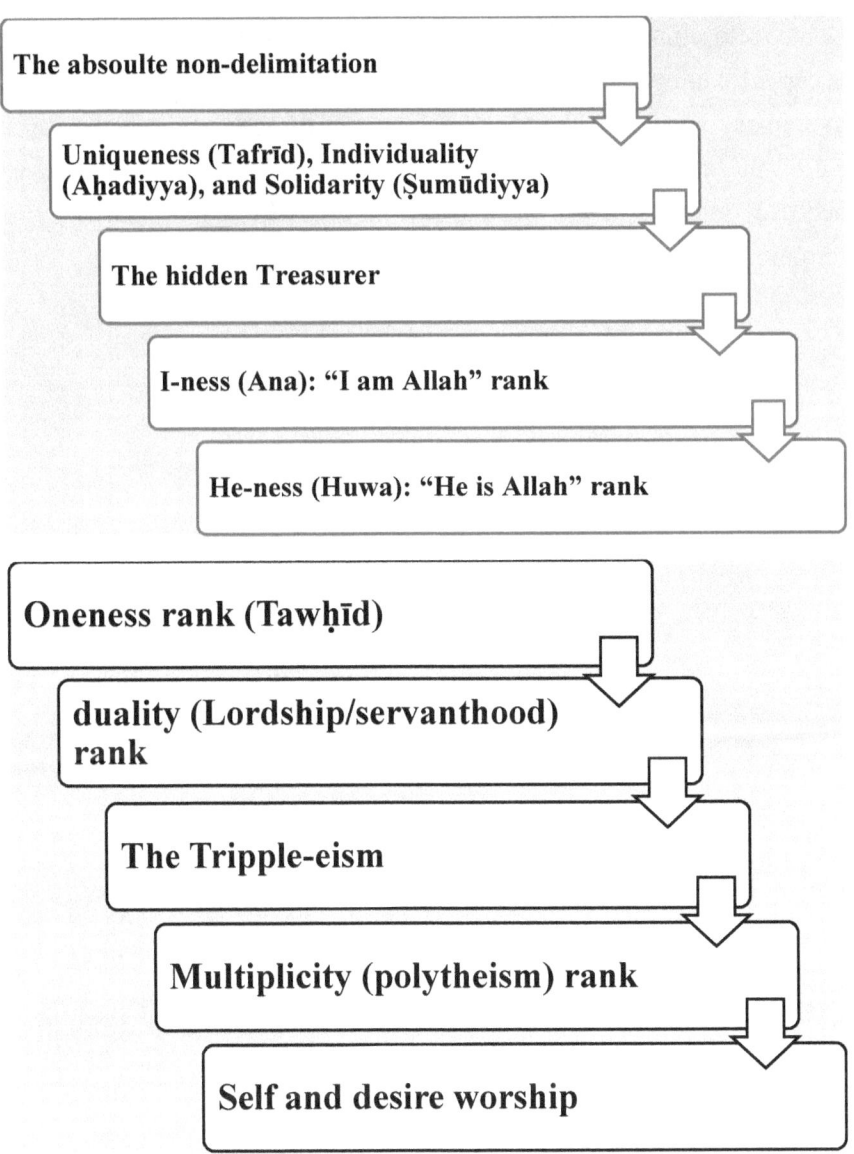

Figure 1 The divine flow transcendence

In the following chapter, I will address the phase of Lordship that was accepted duality. To understand Lordship, Allah revealed multiple exemplary scenes in the Qur'ān. The top of the scenic hierarchy is called the atomic phase scene. To understand the atomic phase, we need to understand the pre-atomic phase, which includes the pre-thinghood.

Chapter 2
"Lordship-Servanthood dialogue: Perception of the Divine Word"

Allah is very near to us. As He describes, He is closer to us than the jugular vein, and *The* Apparent (Al-Dhahir) is one of His names. Additionally, He said that He talked to Musa in words:

"And Allah spoke to Moses with [direct] speech." (Q An-Nisa 164).

There are three means of communicating with God, each with different levels of conception and perception. The tools of conception are the senses, mind, and heart, and the levels are the physical, spiritual, and invincible worlds:

"And it is not for any human being that Allah should speak to him except by revelation or from behind a partition or that He sends a messenger to reveal, by His permission, what He wills. Indeed, He is Most High and Wise." (Q Ash-Shura 51).

In addition, communication with God has a vertical aspect, with lower materialistic perception through the lower self and higher divine perception through God Himself. The holy Hadith demonstrates the higher divine communication:

"I become his eye by which he can see, his ear by which he can hear, his foot by which he can walk, and his hand by which he can wave and move." (Hadith Qudsi).

Lordship transcendence is mentioned in an authentic Hadith, which states that our Lord descends to the first heaven in the last third of the night. According to this belief, Allah created the heavens and the earth as a massive tablet that reflects the microcosmic nature of humankind, with the hearts being the location of ultimate reality and the place for divine secrets. The mind is given sovereignty over the senses, and humans are directed to reverse this cycle. The journey of ascendance from servanthood starts with controlling the senses and thoughts, which is necessary to control mind errors. It ultimately opens a gate to the layers and veils of the heart, leading to the divine secret inside the heart.

This inverted universe inside the human being makes it straightforward to clairvoyant individuals that the transcendence of lordship and servanthood occurs inside the heart, and all the actions of the universe serve as a massive educational tablet or blackboard that demonstrate daily lessons in a classroom style. The ascendant penetration into the sky of this 'allusive construct we call the universe' requires a vehicle, a pilot, guiding illumination signs, knowledge of what to do and what not to do a pathway, and a purpose. The ultimate objective of creating this system of possibilities and capabilities is to teach the offspring of Adam their journey toward the reality inside their hearts.

The critical question arises: What is the purpose of the sun, moon, stars, and planets that Allah repeatedly described as signs? Do they exist to showcase Allah's tremendous capabilities, or do they have an educational role in the universe's classroom?

Levels of Perceivers of the Divine Word:

1. **The Arrogant:** Scholarly individuals at the level of the book's perception favor Scripture-based knowledge, relying on reading, memorizing, recalling, comparing opinions, and then rephrasing and paraphrasing. This group theoretically

accepts the existence of allyhood but restricts it to certain past times or departed people. According to the definition, allyhood (Wilaya) is a unique special selection of God for certain people at the top of the spiritual hierarchy. This allyhood status is combined with specific gifts from God that define them. Allah has chosen certain groups of humankind to be the richest and others to be the healthiest or the most powerful. This also applies to the spiritual hierarchy, which has allyhood and God's allies at the top.

2. **The Mocking People:** Non-allyhood believers perceive God's word as only a written word. These are the people of the letters. This group is partially literate, perceives God's word through a materialistic livelihood lens, and selectively accepts some recognized scholars' opinions. They reject what seems illogical and usually mock those who believe in God's friendship, i.e., the allyhood believers.

3. **The Oppressed Yet Transgressors:** This group has a low allyhood acceptance level of perception and may perceive God's word in more depth than the former two groups, but they are not polished by the wisdom of a 'Good Servant' who would educate and train them. That group is at considerable risk of being gently oppressed and falling into con artists' and conning women's traps. The group members stay tangled in the cobwebs of the former two groups. They cannot immigrate away physically or mentally from the soft mind control or speech glamour of the scholarly or mockery groups: "When the angels seize the souls of those who have wronged themselves—scolding them, 'What was wrong with you?' they will reply, 'We were oppressed in the land.' The angels will respond, 'Was Allah's earth not spacious enough for you

to emigrate?' It is they who will have Hell as their home. What an evil destination." (Q An-Nisa 97).

4. **The Deniers:** The non-guru-based wayfarer level of perception may start with spiritual openings but may end with arrogant self-image, biased thinking, and delusional ideation. This results in denying the message carrier messenger of their community or God's ally of their time. Subsequently, they fall into the darkness of Satan (Taghoot):

   "We surely sent a messenger to every community, saying, 'Worship Allah and shun false gods.' But Allah guided some of them, while others were destined to stray. So travel throughout the land and see the fate of the deniers." (Q An-Nahl 36).

   They may even make their denial a revenue-generating tool and gradually become devil's advocates:

   "And make your provision that you deny?" (Q Al-Waqia 82).

5. **The Misguided:** A misguided guru-based level of perception of the divine word group usually has a guru from the literalist first or partially literalist second group, who lacks illuminated wisdom, and their source of knowledge is searching and regurgitating the old folks' books. This perception of the divine word of this group never exceeds some old interpretations of departed authentic (during their time) gurus. This is a hard-working group, yet their efforts are wasted and do not add value to Gnosticism:

   "Say (O Muhammad SAW): 'Shall We tell you the greatest losers in respect of (their) deeds? Those whose efforts have

11

been wasted in this life while they thought that they were acquiring good by their deeds.'" (Q Kahf 103–104).

6. The Wanderers of an Authentic Sheikh/Guru Perceivers: The divine word is received before it dwells in scripted letters' destination. This showcases the superiority paradox of the so-called illiterates (Um'miyeen) compared to the literates:

   "He is the One Who raised for the illiterate 'people' a messenger from among themselves—reciting His revelations, purifying them, and teaching them the Book and wisdom, for indeed they had previously been astray." (Q Al-Jumu'a 2).

   They perceive the word or the message in dreams, awake visions, or tangibly. Dreams are primarily symbolic, and every detail counts and may represent passing over to the world of symbolism before materializations into tangible occurrences but may also represent the translation of a person's thoughts or intentions. Awake visions are achieved through meditation and approved by the sheikh, who possesses expertise and knowledge. Awake visions of shapes, formulas, solids, colors, or light also need education and interpretation. If the seeker has an opening in hearing, the word could be heard through an internal voice (Hatef). If the opening is in the hand, the seeker can feel it; if the opening is on the foot, the seeker can travel without leaving his place.

7. **The Spoken-To People (Muhaddathoon):** This is a soul dialogue. This may resemble how the scripted words or sentences descend directly or collectively to the heart of the prophets. A wayfarer gifted a taste of this divine word-level perception would acquire what others acquire after decades of studying in minutes of revelation and disclosure. This unique

perception of the sacred word from the breath, the eternal sea wave motion, the embodied travelers called Hajeer. The embodied traveler then takes the seeker to the imagery traces of the initial word. I may dedicate a chapter about the Hajeer and its unique way of perceiving God's word. But the classic example of Hajeer is when Maryam perceives Allah's word as a perfect human. The initial meeting with the Hajeer is likened to the initial three squeezes by the angel Gabriel to the Prophet (PBUH).

Chapter 3
"Unveiling Divinity through Humankind's Creation"

Section 1: From Dust to Trust

The Holy Phase of Humankind's Origin

In the Surah of Humankind (al-*Insān*), Allah reveals that humankind's origin is mysterious, pure, and subtle, beyond complete description:

"Has there come upon the human being a period when he was nothing to be mentioned?" (Q Insān 1).

Despite this mystery, humanity's holy phase (al-marḥala al-qudsiyya) exists within the divine sea of praise, remembrance, and expression. Acts such as praising, remembering, recalling, and expressing are all forms of worship, as reflected in the saying, *"No one worships Allah but Allah Himself."* This aligns with the verse: *"I only created jinn and humankind to worship Me." Q Adh-Dhariyat 56).* Thus, this holy phase can be likened to a preconception phase preceding an embryo in the womb, whose only activities are nourishment and immersion in amniotic fluid—a phase forgotten upon birth. In this way, Allah mirrors the story of creation in the process of human preconception, conception and birth, starting from an idea in the minds of parents. This "preconceived" idea—the wordplay is intentional—can be likened to humanity's holy phase, which precedes the physical stages of the embryo, the newborn child, and each stage of development.

Following this ineffable holy phase, humankind became determined as a distinct entity, thus entering the phase of "thing-hood" (marḥalat al-shay'iyya). This phase, described in verse 2 of the same Surah, involved the use of clay, fire, water, and air to create human beings: *"We created the human being from a drop of mixed fluid, to test him; and We made him hearing and seeing"* (Q Insān 2). Clay is a flexible and moldable medium that reflects a specific aspect of ultimate reality: divine flow. Fire symbolizes transformation and energy, while water represents life and sustenance. Finally, air embodies the breath of life, connecting the physical and spiritual realms. Together, these elements contribute to the essence of humanity, illustrating the complexity and richness of human existence.

Having been defined as a distinct entity, Allah equipped a divine flow—this divine presence within humankind—with the ability to hear and see (Q Insān 2). This flow perceives divine traces in scattered dispersion (al-furqān), signifying a transition from the gnosis of divinity's exclusive singularity (aḥadiyya) to the duality of Lord and servant in Lordship. The faculties of hearing and seeing encompass both positive and negative aspects: they mark a connection to and a separation from the divine. Our earthly reality invites us to seek knowledge and to look beyond what is immediately evident, yet it veils us from the luminous beyond.

Beings are merely dimensional shapes of the command of Lordship "Be." Beings are commanded to breath that was permitted to have boundaries made of different mixes of the four elements of dust, air, fire, and, most importantly, water. Subsequently, beings mature as external shells that vary in dryness, wetness, coolness, and warmth. According to the ancient science of numerology, the mathematical reference number for the word "Be" (konn) in Arabic is 20 (kaf) + 50 (noon) = 70. The mathematical combination code of the four elements, multiplied 70 times, is exponential, and so are the variation

15

possibilities of the manifestations of the divine secret contained by the beings' shells.

The pre-dust (pre-atomic) swimming phase:

This is the second subtle, hidden, and unrevealed preconceived phase that follows the Holy phase. The concept of pre-creation suggests that everything was once hidden knowledge within Allah's unlimited and indefinite knowledge. Since Allah created Adam in His image, it is permissible to use the image of Adam as a metaphor to understand the idea. It is as though we are thoughts in a single human mind, data in an unlimited database, or drops of water in a vast ocean. Each data point or water drop is given partial artificial intelligence capabilities to learn about others. Although the drops and data are very similar, their way of learning is limited to a specific perspective or path of perception, which cannot be exceeded. This limitation is referred to as the "orbit."

Each piece of data has a specific orbit, and these orbits have divine boundaries (ḥudūd-Allāh) that should never be crossed. As part of the educational strategy, these pieces of data are given the ability to exceed the divine boundaries, but doing so leads to an agnostic character and drowning in the dark sea of unknown, non-manifest names (bāṭin names) or what is not allowed to be known. Sailing in the ocean of unseen knowledge without a guide results in confusion.

These data points exist in pairs because Allah's names are balanced. Therefore, these paired data, in one scene, swim in the divine non-delimitation, centered around primordial light (the Muḥammadian or praising light). As Allah describes, the praising light is also paired as the illuminating lamp (sirāj munīr), a paired quality of the sun and the moon.

This is a spiritual phase that devoted individuals can experience during meditation. The ultimate goal is to progress from returning to God, represented by only three letters of the divine name (الله), to *being returned* to God and fulfilling the first letter (the letter Alif "اً") in the journey. Achieving this phase involves navigating through a straight-line ocean of theological non-delimitation by swimming (*subḥān*) in a sea of light.

This divine orbital swimming, with a warning against drowning in the non-manifested ocean, is beautifully declared in Surah Yasin. You may taste such understanding if you read the verses from Surah Yaseen (36-43) within the abovementioned context."

36. Glory be to He, who created all the pairs of whatever the earth grows, of themselves, and of what they do not know.

37. Another sign for them is the night: We strip the day from it—and they are in darkness.

38. And the sun runs its course towards its destined point. That is the design of the Almighty, the All-Knowing.

39. And the moon: We have disposed of it in phases—until it returns like the old twig.

40. The sun is not to overtake the moon, nor is the night to outpace the day. Each glides in an orbit.

41. Another sign for them is that We carried their ancestors in the loaded Ark.

42. And We created for them the like of it, in which they ride.

43. If We willed, We could drown them—with no screaming to be heard from them, nor will they be saved.

The concept of paired individuals is illustrated in different scenarios. For example, angels surrounding Adam and Eve are permissible and beautiful. At the same time, Satan is a vindictive one to avoid. Every paired soul knows Allah if it stays within its boundaries and abides by its Dos and don'ts.

The ultimate manifestation of the paired individuals is when they gather on Earth. They will hear Satan giving his disclosures in a speech.

"And Satan will say when the matter has been concluded, "Indeed, Allah had promised you the promise of truth. And I promised you, but I betrayed you. But I had no authority over you except that I invited you, and you responded to me. So I don't think you should blame me for this, but blame yourselves. I cannot be called to your aid, nor can you be called to my aid. Indeed, I deny your association of me [with Allah] before. Indeed, for the wrongdoers are in a painful punishment." (*Q* Ibrahim 22).

They then face what they deny: calling their partners, who created themselves, without response. They will learn then that the centrality of kingship belongs to the one and compeller. "The Day when they will emerge, nothing about them is hidden from Allah. "To whom does sovereignty belong today?" *"To Allah, the One, the Irresistible."* (*Q* Ghafer 16).

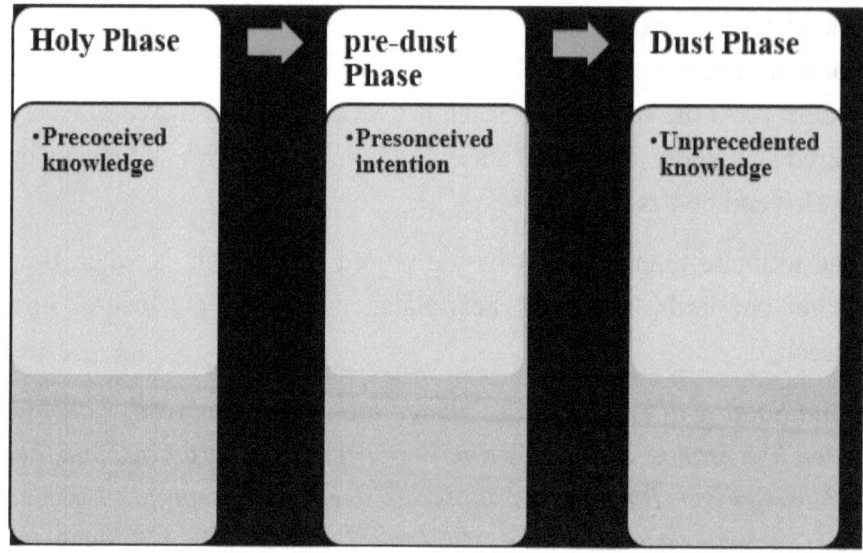

Holy Phase	pre-dust Phase	Dust Phase
•Precoceived knowledge	•Presonceived intention	•Unprecedented knowledge

Figure 2: The Preceocoception Phases

The dust (minute) Phase (Alam Al-Dharr):

In the atomic phase, the descendants of the concept of divinity progress from denying any partners or creations to recognizing creation as traces of the manifestation of divine names, attributes, and essence. These subtle beings are granted the ability to see and hear. Once they acquire these faculties, they are immediately asked, "Am I not your Lord?" They respond, "Yes, You are," thereby declaring their recognition of Lordship. The subtle atoms illuminate and answer, "Yes, we do," in the purest form of acknowledging the Creator's Lordship. This phase is characterized by uniformity and non-differentiation, lacking intellectual discourse or mental development. It represents the purest and most credible phase of recognizing Lordship:

19

"And when Your Lord summoned the descendants of Adam, and He made them testify about themselves, 'Am I not your Lord?' They said, 'Yes, You are, we testify.' Thus, you cannot say on the Day of Resurrection, 'We were unaware of this.' Nor can you say, 'Our ancestors practiced idolatry before, and we are their descendants who came after them. Will You destroy us for what the falsifiers have done?" (Q Aa'raaf 172–173).

Following the recognition and declaration by the atoms, Allah warns of the next phase: the revelation of the secret of Lordship, which is the Adamic prototypic phase.

The thing-hood phase:

The next phase of humankind, the thing-hood phase, required the density of clay, fire, water, and air to create human beings. Clay provides a flexible, mouldable medium that can demonstrate a specific aspect of the ultimate reality: divine flow.

Allah equipped this flow of divine presence with the ability to become hearing and seeing their traces in dispersion (Furqan) so they can evolve from the gnosis of individuality (Ahadiya) to the duality of Lordship/servanthood.

 Hearing and seeing have positive and negative aspects because our earthly reality should lead us to seek knowledge and look beyond what is immediately evident." *We created the human being from a drop of mixed fluid, to test him; and We made him hearing and seeing" (Q Insan 2)*

This holy-like phase immerses oneself in the divine sea of praise, remembrance, and expression. Praising, remembering, mentioning, recalling, and expressing are all forms of worship. This is what the saying means: No one worships Allah but Allah Himself. *"I did not create jinn and humans except to worship Me"* (Q Adhariyat 56)

This phase can be likened to an embryo in the mother's womb, where the embryo's only activities are eating and swimming in the amniotic fluid. The embryo ultimately forgets this phase upon birth. Allah has mirrored the story of creation in the process of human conception and birth, evolving from a mere idea in the minds of parents to one phase to another.

The trust phase:

Interactions in the divine flow leave traces. However, only the purest traces can reveal and teach about the events of divine flow transcendence beyond illusions, especially in humanity and specifically in the descendants of Adam, the messengers, prophets, and allies of Allah.

During this learning process, from being an original drop of fluid to becoming knowledgeable traces, the purity of these traces is lost when they penetrate the barriers of others.

The return journey begins at the lowest point, which Allah designates as grade 1 schooling. Successful traces return to their original form of knowledge rather than aimlessly wandering. They can be described as becoming pure again.

During the return journey, they leave traces of gold, fruit, trees, innocent children, and pure women in the heavens, while others leave traces of fire, lava, beasts, reptiles, and poisons.

Additionally, they are given the means of guidance (minds) that can translate perceived knowledge into understandable images and the ability to complement each other's knowledge; *"We guided him to the way, be he appreciative or unappreciative"* (Q Insan 3).

A mind must inherently possess both certainty and doubt as guidance. By "mind," I do not mean the brain matter. Every atom of a human being contains a small mind. However, these minds have numerous pathways, and the brain serves as a standard stop. The brain should not be the final destination; otherwise, there would be no guidance.

This lesson was demonstrated to Adam through a forbidden tree, with Satan representing the alternative reality outside of exploration, as warned by Allah.

"Don't (approach) get in the proximity of this tree" (Q Baqaraa 35).

The final destination should be the heart. The heart is an invisible, subtle cavitary compartment that contains Allah's divine secret and treasure box. Allah described this hidden cavitary compartment: *"My earth and my sky never contained me. However, the heart of my believing servant does." (Ghazali, Ihyaa)*

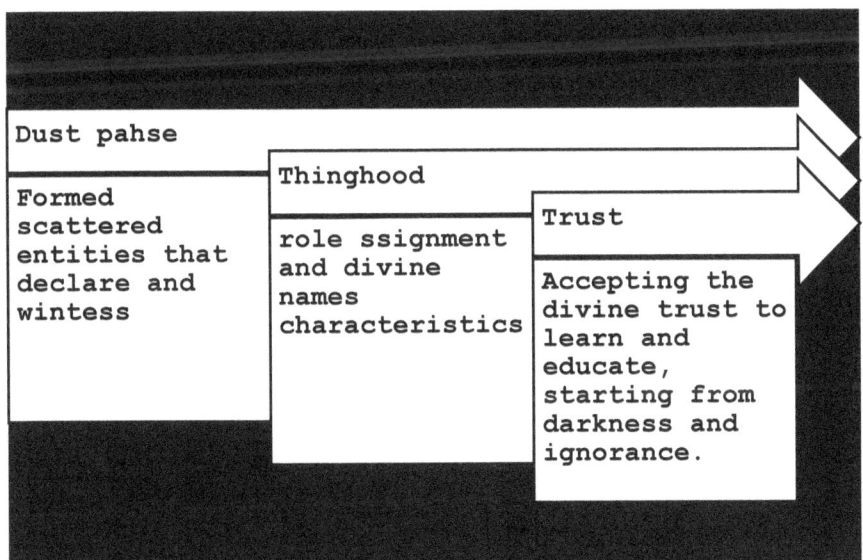

The Adamic Scene and Inauguration Phase:

In the Adamic scene and inauguration phase, a step-down process involves various "actors," including angels, Adam (representing centrality and ultimate knowledge), and Satan (representing ignorance). Adam, as the central figure, embodies a denser vessel for divine light.

"When your Lord said to the angels, "I am placing a successor on earth." They said, "Will You place in it someone who will work corruption in it and shed blood while we declare Your praises and sanctify You?" He said, "I know what you do not know." And He taught Adam the names, all of them. Then He presented them to the angels and said, "Tell Me the names of these if you are truthful." They said, "Glory be to You! We have no knowledge except what You have taught us. It is you who are the All-Knowing, the All-Wise. He said, "O Adam, inform them of their names.". And when he informed them of their names, He said, "Did I not tell you that I know the secrets of the heavens and the earth and that I know what you disclose and what you did conceal?". We said to the angels, "Prostrate to Adam." So, they prostrated, except for Iblis. He refused, acted arrogantly, and became one of the disbelievers. (Q Baqarah 30-34)

Adam was considered a representation of divine light infused into a vessel made of clay. He was like a statue given life and the ability to express and explain, revealing the secrets of Allah's name. Hence, the angels' prostration was a command to acknowledge the manifestations of the creator's names within Adam. In other words, Adam represented the meanings and attributes simply by being himself. He was a multi-dimensional, eloquent, and expressive educational construct. This educational phase allowed for denial by Satan and internal questioning by the angels. It permitted the evolution of imagery, the unveiling of comprehension, and the allowance of decision-making without consequences. Therefore, this phase was less pure and more educational through differentiation. It's important not to forget the initial prime light centrality of the atomic phase. Everything that follows is the flow and dispersion of the secret of the primordial light within creation. This educational phase demonstrates the unlimited and indefinite capabilities of the pre-atomic phase's primordial, divine light centrality.

The post-descendance to Earth phase:

This is often referred to as the lower life or (Al-hayatul-doniya), and is relatively short and educational compared to the Other day or the hereafter, which is long and compelling. The senses that are primarily external, elusive, and soothing, in contrast with the more realistically revealing senses from the other day.

The Transitional Night Phase:

Often described as a night in the grave due to the prevailing darkness when the body is returned to Mother Earth, the senses are primarily internal and resemble the awakened senses of a lifetime of sleep. They may become aware of the people above Earth, but may not be capable of direct communication or impact.

The Gathering Scene (Earth of Gathering):

This is referred to as the other day in the Quran (Alyawm Al-a`kher), the other life (Al-hayat-ul-`akhera), or the hereafter. *"They are` the ones who favour the lower life of this world over the Hereafter and hinder `others` from the Way of Allah, striving to make it crooked. It is they who have gone far astray."* (Q Ibrahim 3).

It begins after human beings awaken from their night in the graves, gaining different senses that perceive their surroundings in unique ways during an initial phase of hereafter lordship, and revelation afterlife. This happens when the mountains disappear, another gigantic, flat, extended earth emerges, and all creatures are gathered in lines. They are reminded that they claimed this time would never come. This is showcased in Surah Al-Kahf 47–50:

47. "On the Day when We set the mountains in motion, and you see the earth emerging, We gather them together and leave none behind."

48. "They will be presented before your Lord in a row. 'You have come to Us as We created you the first time. Although you claimed We would not set an appointment for you.'"

49. "And the book will be placed, and you will see the guilty fearful of its contents. And they will say, 'Woe to us! What is with this book that leaves nothing, small or big, but it has enumerated it?' They will find everything they have done present. Your Lord never wrongs anyone."

50. "We said to the angels, 'Prostrate before Adam.' So they prostrated, except for Iblis. He was of the jinn and deviated from the command of his Lord. Will you take him and his descendants as friends instead of Me, although they are your enemy? What an evil alternative for the wrongdoers!" (Q Kahf 47–50).

Unlike in the initial atomic phase, when certainty was the dominant theme, doubt now reigns supreme. It will be apparent to them that they were gathered in the same manner as when they were initially created.

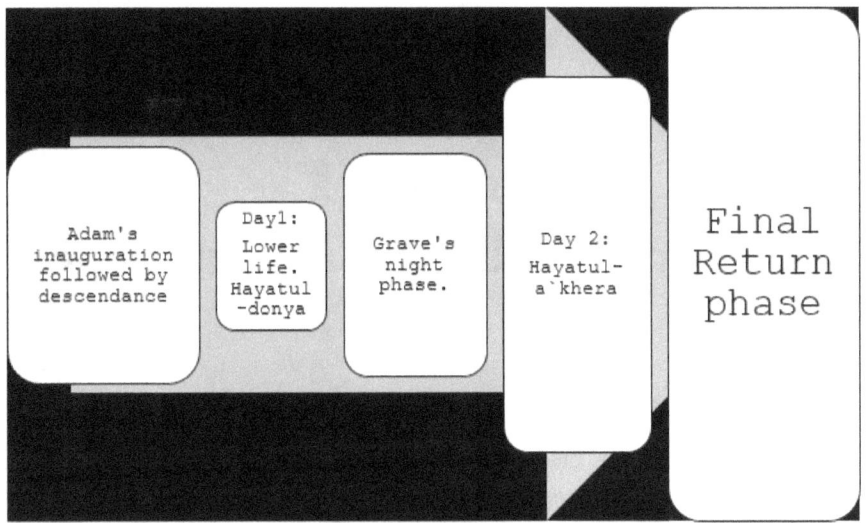

Figure 4: Humankind's thinghood phases and return journey

Chapter 4
"The Revelation of Lordship through the Human 'Self'
The diversive, collective, and one Selves"

Gathering one's Selves:

The Quran frequently discusses the Self as an intricate, unique entity, sparking deep curiosity about its nature and purpose. Is the self unifaceted or multifaceted? What roles does it play? Are we defined by our physical form, inner being, or both? What influences the self's inclinations? How can we elevate and, as the Quran suggests, cleanse our "selves"? These questions inspire a profound exploration of the self and its potential for growth and enlightenment.

Knowing the self is a critical step in understanding Lordship.

"The one who knows himself knows his Lord" is considered by some to be an authentic prophetic quote. This quote suggests that the self, similar to the spirit (Rouh), is a disclosure phase of Lordship or the ultimate destination of the descent of Lordship from highness to lowliness, reflecting in the servant's self-reflecting heart tablet. In the list of stages in the divine flow of transcendence, it is essential to note that as you delve deeper, you encounter a more detailed understanding of the concept. This leads to increased varied perspectives and detailed observations. However, it's crucial to remain cautious, as this complexity can lead to losing sight of unity, unification (Tawheed), and individuality (Tafreed). Some describe this as the wayfaring self-struggle, and the difficulties imposed by the "clay" component of the wayfarer create a muddy nature of the path from duality to oneness (Tawheed). The individual self-struggle is likened to cutting through a muddy walking path. Therefore, the evolutionary definition of the self is that the self is a lower manifestation of the soul's devolution during the descent of the divine flow.

This suggests that once one loses hold of duality and delves more deeply, the path becomes muddied, often referred to as the muddy phase of oneness (Awhal Altawheed).

The self in the duality phase is a pure and enlightened essence originating directly from a divine and sacred soul. This beautiful mirror image of the pure self and the holy soul best describes the Muhammadian self and Allah's soul (Ruhullah). It's important to note that Allah's soul is not the essence of Allah, nor is it the source of life for God, as God is eternally self-sufficient. Instead, it represents the profound and subtle essence of divine power veiled within the function of Lordship.

Humankind may become overwhelmed by the capabilities this self affords them, leading them to act 'selfish'—a wordplay that is intentional. Being selfish causes them to claim ownership of this subtle phase of Lordship, transforming them into their own Lords. Consequently, they reject the laws mandated by the creator that are meant to protect them from this importing Lordship pitfall.

Conversely, those who manage to evade this trap are awarded the highest title of being **servants**.

*"There they found a **servant** of Ours, to whom We had granted mercy from Us and enlightened with the knowledge of Our Own"* (Q Kahf 65).

*"Glory be to the One Who took His **servant** by night from the Sacred Mosque to the Farthest Mosque whose surroundings We have blessed, so that We may show him some of Our signs"* (Q Israa' 1).

Allah has graciously exemplified this wisdom through the creation of the archangel Gabriel and the remarkable human embodiment of the soul, Jesus, the son of Mary. Jesus is described as the Soul of Allah (Ruhullah) and His Word. Jesus beautifully manifested both the Soul of Allah and the commanding word in human form. However, it's crucial to understand that Jesus symbolized and embodied the secret of the divine soul and the commanding word rather than representing Lordship or divinity. Instead, he represented a magnificent sub-evolution of the Lordship's command, as emphasized in the Quran as the commanding word "be."

The Muhammadian self (Nafs Muhammadiyah) represents the pure, original version of the human being (Fitra), or in biological terms, the original chromosome. Other aspects of the self are acquired through parents, actions, societal norms, and cultures. Throughout life, we accumulate additional elements to the self, some of which may not align with our ideals, shaped by harmful desires, indulgence, greed, or other lower inclinations. These additional aspects are considered "newbies" (Muhdathat), and we must eliminate them through good deeds or seeking forgiveness.

The Muhammadian self is within us, as suggested by a high-level interpretation of the Quranic verse:

"Know that Allah's Messenger is within you" (*Q* Hujorat 7).

"Indeed, a messenger has come to you from within yourselves" (Q Attawba 128).

The added self-level that evolves at puberty is a collective self comprising the Muhammadian self and additional acquired traits. Since every reality represents living conscious beings, multifaceted, customized selves emerge as long as the agglomerative self controls the external senses.

- Self, similar to Spirit (Rouh), is a subtle phase of Lordship disclosure.

- The self acts as an internal messenger that educates, guides, hints, and warns.

- Humankind contributes an abundance of deficient copies of the self (the Divisive Selfs).

- The agglomertive self is the purest truth seeker he/she could be with cleansing practices.

- The agglomertative self role is to fetch the treasure of the Fitra messenger within.

- The purest self is enclosed within the natural essence (Fitra). The truth se

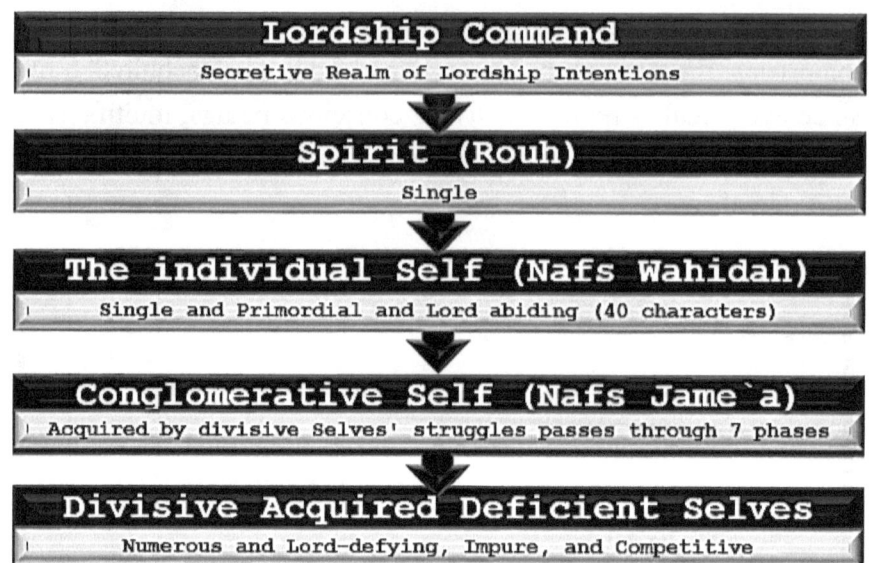

Figure: Disclosure of the lordship command from Spirit to Self

The Agglomerative Self's Exploration of Divisive Selves:

Understanding the agglomerative self involves studying the divisive selves. This understanding is attained by allowing the internal senses to control the inner vision rather than relying on the external vision. The internal vision is esoteric, enabling communication and learning from the various aspects of the divisive selves, primarily through observation (Mushahada), and potentially through other senses such as feeling and speaking. Opening the internal heart's sight is usually subtle and gradual, transitioning from lower to higher understanding. This process is called disclosure (Kashf), while sudden, overwhelming revelation is referred to as Divine manifestation (Tajalli) instead of the top-down compelling approach.

During meditation, a person looks inward with closed eyes, as if the agglomerative self, like a complex single cluster, breaks into smaller mini-clusters in a top-down manner. The primary objective of the agglomerative self is to gather all knowledge and experience about the other selves and return to its pure Muhammadian self. This is achieved through meditation and self-observation. Transitioning from a fragmented cluster of selves to a unified self that acknowledges and embodies its purest Muhammadian self is the destination for "the gathering" (Al-Jam 'e). It represents a significant step toward recognizing one's spiritual essence.

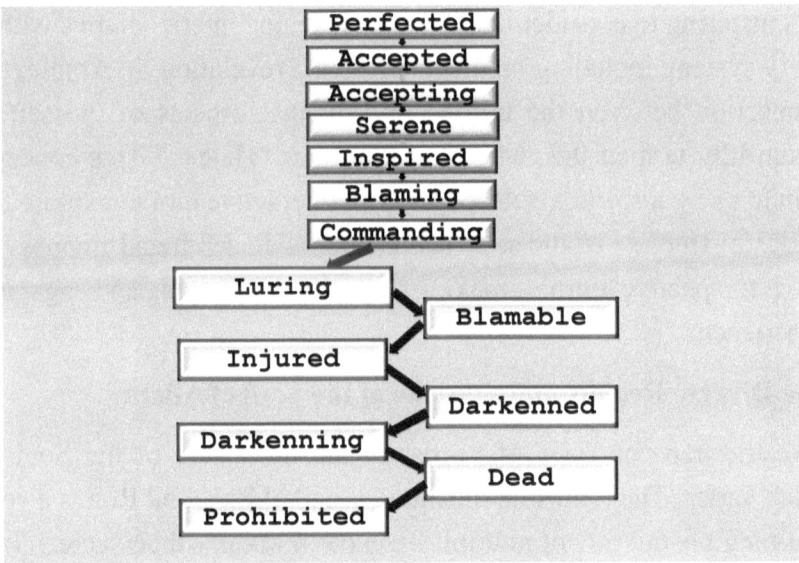

Figure: Phases of the Conglomerative Self from Evil to Goodness

The Quran begins with the powerful seven-verse chapter known as the Mother of the Book or Fatiha, setting the stage for a profound and enlightening journey through its other verses:

"And a Quran which We have divided so that you might recite it to men at intervals. And We have revealed it in stages" (Q Israa 106).

> - The Fatiha (the Opening of the Book or the Mother of the Book) exemplifies the agglomerative self, while the remainder of the Quran's verses represent pure noncompeting divisive selves. Whereas the first dot of the first letter of the Fatiha (The Dot of the Ba) represents the Spirit

The journey of self-learning and self-discovery, known as "the division" (Furqan), is a transformative process guided by divine revelation or manifestation. This empowering journey transcends the limitations of the mind, enabling personal growth and understanding.

It is inspiring to consider that Allah has created intermediaries within every system, including moments of divine revelation. In Arabic, the connection between the unified and distinct aspects of the self is beautifully termed the "Migrating Soul" or "Hajeer." This concept, akin to using a spiritual telescope, is an interactive tool to explore the intricate structure of the self. The Hajeer adds depth and richness to this introspective journey, making it a truly enlightening and engaging experience.

The Diverse Realms and Stations of the Soul of Allah:

Like the transcendence of Lordship, the disclosure of the Soul of Allah varies. The term soul in Arabic is called Roh, and Roh is a very non-tangible mixture of multiple essences that carry their secrets. It is likened to the combined scent of numerous roses and flowers. So, we can say that Roh is a secret of the secrets of God's names or attributes. Roh can quickly diffuse and penetrate barriers and go through things. Roh is pure and free from defects. The Soul of Allah is permitted to be disclosed following Lordship's command. Therefore, soul disclosure follows a unique pathway, providing an elegant intermediary for the divine dialogue called inspiration (Wahy).

For any central reality in the universe, God has created living beings who become the reflection of such a reality and an opposite evil image to showcase the reality of opposition. The Soul was represented in creation by Jesus (PBUH) among humankind and by Gabriel, the master angel among the angels. The evil opposite of the soul is the False Messiah or the Antichrist, who will appear in the last days. The evil opposites of Gabriel are the outcast angels Harut and Marut.

The transcendence of the soul is exemplified by the vertical movement of Gabriel with the Quran upon the Prophet (PBUH), by the descent of the perfect human spirit upon Mary to give her immaculate conception, and by the ascension of Jesus to reside in the second heaven.

The practical meaning of prophecy:

The Spirit descends, impacts, and reveals the Lordship's command.

The Lordship commands.

The spirit descends on the servant heart and being during meditation.

The initial embrace and constriction.

The recipient is gathered in a tight embrace.

The recipient's external awareness may either vanish partially or entirely.

The display of images, travel, conversations, questions and answers, or the descent of letters and sentences on the servant's internal horizon.

Return to the physical worldly senses.

Translating the message.

Sharing the message with others (prophecy).

The Cascade of transition of Divine Sacred Intention:

1. Divinity's presence through meditation
2. The ocean (Divine Ocean of hidden knowledge).
3. Exalted Lord.
4. Lordship Data (Tablet and Pen Data).
5. Command.
6. Commanding Word.
7. Spirit descent.
8. Immigrating companion (Hajeer).
9. The Human Heart.
10. Mind.
11. Images.
12. Interpretation.
13. Voiced Word.
14. Scripted Word.
15. Humankind's transference of divine knowledge
16. Human attempts against evil interception of the Receding Whisperer.
17. People's hearts.
18. People's minds.
19. Mass understanding.

The Hajeer (The Immigrating Being):

To understand the Hajeer concept, it's essential to explain that there is a series of hidden spiritual events before the divine message is revealed in written or spoken form. The message begins as a divine will, a command, a "be" word, and ultimately manifests through a being who delivers the message to His people. These messengers carry the same message from one form to another until it reaches the Adamic human servant during his meditation and solitude with God.

Thus, it's essential to notice that the messenger is disclosed before the message or that the messenger is the exact essence of the message. Historically, the appearance of Prophet Muhammad (PBUH) preceded the revelation of the Quran, as if he were the embodied teachings of the Quran, as described by his beloved wife, Aisha.

The message cascade takes different forms, each as a link to the next. For instance, Archangel Gabriel represented the Hajeer of the Quran before delivering its words. In other words, Gabriel introduced the Prophet Muhammad (PBUH) to his unified and divisive selves in terms of Quranic chapters and verses.

This sets the stage for the Hajeer to serve as an intermediate form of the messenger before transforming into the message itself. The recipient of the message from the Hajeer is responsible for interpreting it in various forms and manifestations. The human expression of this message is often met with objections and denials regarding its content or the process through which it was obtained.

Chapter 5
"Salat:
The Lordship-Servanthood Link"

Salat = Link = Lordship-Servanthood Connection

People often refer to Salat as prayer. However, the linguistic meaning of Salat is a link or connection. Salat is described in the Quran as a "Temporal Book." Combining both meanings suggests that the outward performance of a prayer should internally connect you to divine knowledge.

"Indeed, the prayer is, for the believers, a timed book"

(Q An-Nisa 103).

The revelation of the Book of Salat is multi-dimensional, encompassing literal, definite, and functional dimensions, among others. The Quran's literal dimension is linguistically dependent. However, Allah indicated the existence of other books within the Quran that are worth exploring. As Allah mentions the wise book (Ketab Hakeem) and the self-explanatory book (Ketab Mobeen), He also refers to Salat (prayer) as a time-tabled book:

Therefore, Salat is embedded within the Quran (The Book). But what is Salat? Is it merely the ritualistic external movements associated with reciting quotes from the Quran?

The Quran describes *Salat* as a book. To understand its content, we need to "open" this book. Is it readable, audible, or memorable—perhaps even all of these? How is this book categorized? Does it fall under history, literature, science, meditation, or another category? What is the proper way to read this book? Lastly, and most importantly, are the terms *Salat* and prayer interchangeable?

Interpreting Salat in the Quran simply as 'prayer' can be misleading; it encompasses much more. Prayer is just one aspect of this rich practice.

Prayer is a ritual that involves external movements, specific intentions, goals, and recitations that reflect certain ideologies. The closest Arabic term for prayer is the performance of Salat (Qadaa *Salat*). The primary objectives of prayer or Salat are intentional and can encompass requests for tangible and intangible desires. Additionally, individuals may perform prayer as an obligatory ritual (*Fard*) in gratitude for the blessings bestowed by the Lord, or they may engage in additional prayers beyond the required ones. The latter is referred to as supra-obligatory or voluntary prayer (Nafela).

Performing Salat is an act of servanthood that involves preparation, external cleansing, dedicating time, and asking. Through recited words, it captures a dialogue between the worshipper and Allah. This ritual also symbolizes the literal and physical reenactment of the names of Allah (الله) and Muhammad (محمد) in the Arabic script.

The prayer begins with raising both arms forming the shape of '2 lams) (لـل) positioning the whole body in a straight line or 'Alif ' (ا), while the prayer space represents a circle or 'Haa' (ه).

During this act, a fierce battle occurs between two opposing forces fighting over the external senses: the mind and the heart. The mind feels the pain of losing its leadership role as the guiding direction of the senses. It employs various strategies to resist submission. This hidden animosity becomes evident when prayer begins.

While the mind allows some space for humans to hope or wish (*Tamanny*), it views the heart's rebellion as stemming from the external senses. The mind will do whatever it takes to prevent the submission of external senses by generating background chatter that distracts from directing the senses toward the heart's facade.

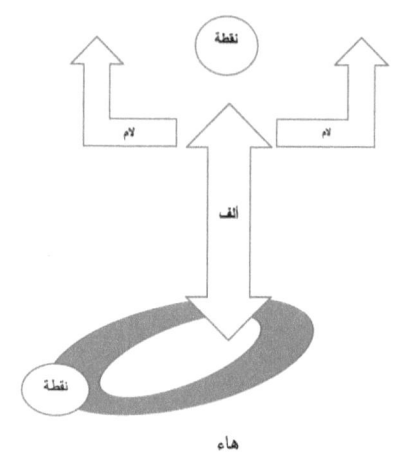

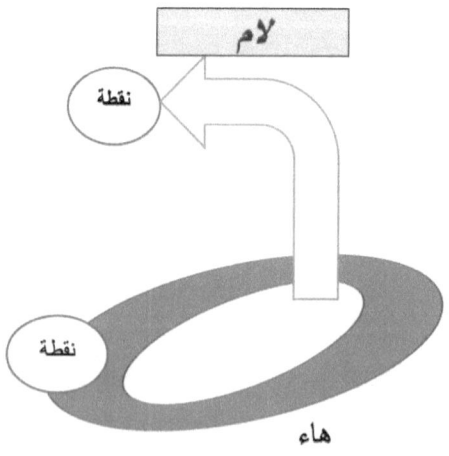

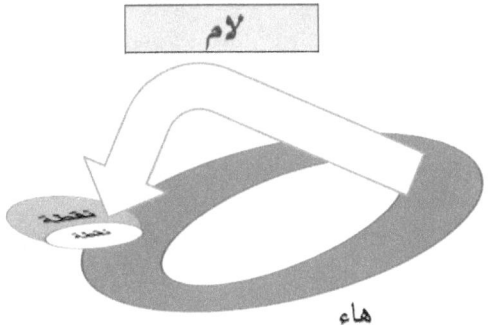

Most of this mental activity occurs outside of prayer. The mind employs hopes, unfulfilled dreams, temporary gratifications, and the embellishment of false heart-like feelings such as pseudo-love and mercy as tools of mass distraction.

These weapons require soldiers and a reward. The most common soldiers are associated with gender and what goes into the stomach, while the most significant rewards are sexual gratification and gluttony. The mind may also seek disinhibition, which can come from substances like alcohol or drugs. Contrary to popular belief, these substances can give the mind a sense of uninhibited control, obscuring the connection to the heart. Alcohol, in particular, liberates the mind from the last remnants of control imposed by the heart.

The heart guides the mind through pure essence and exemplary morality. The Prophet Muhammad (PBUH/HF) stated, "I am sent to complete and perfect exemplary ethics" (Mosnad Ahmad and Bukhari in Adab Mofrad). This is why, in communities that indulge in alcohol, there tends to be a wide variety of moral codes; often, individuals or small groups create their own set of morals. As a result, immorality becomes a relative concept in alcohol-centric cultures. This detachment from the heart's purity over the mindset contributes to a rejection of modesty and encourages behaviors such as nudity, fornication, gambling, and violence. Consequently, the mind often dresses repulsive behaviors in polished language. Fornication becomes love, gambling becomes having fun, and nudity becomes showing personality, etc.

Any simple mind understands that the heart is more powerful than the mind, as the heart holds the secret to the divine treasure. Therefore, any strategic action in this ongoing battle should lead to one outcome: achieving a sense of mind sovereignty over the senses. This ultimate goal is known as "HEADLESSNESS."

The quickest way to reclaim the sovereignty of the heart and eliminate mental impurities is through REMEMBRANCE.

Does performing Salat prevent immoral actions and extraordinary wrongdoings? The answer is yes, but this effect is primarily external and apparent during the ritual's performance.

So, what truly transforms an individual from the inside out? This question leads us into the second chapter of the book on Salat.

Establishing the Connection (Iqamat Salat):

The Quran often refers to "establishing" (Iqama) when discussing salat, which is the ultimate goal of any ritual. But who is the connection with? Is there a sign or proof? Is it a goal, means, or both? These questions—what, how, why, and when—apply to establishing salat just as they do to performing it.

The performance of salat (Qadaa *Salat*) alone rarely leads to a genuine connection as long as the mind dominates, causing a lack of focus.

REMEMBRANCE is the most significant indicator of the heart's victory over distractions.

The REMEMBRANCE indicator of heart victory requires proof that remembrance is executed effectively. This complex cycle of establishing a connection depends on performance, which relies on remembrance. Remembrance needs evidence, and the evidence is the divine connection itself, which can be perplexing.

If remembrance is done effectively, it creates light-producing tracings with each breath. These actual angelic beings become support soldiers, sometimes also referred to as the provision (Maddad).

Establishing that a connection is made involves witnessing the divine light and progressive eradication of darkness, a by-product of the rivalry between the soldiers of illumination and darkness. If there is no light, there is no connection. Without this light, there is no protection from indecency or dishonor. It is as straightforward as that. Establishing—not merely performing—prayer (Salat or the link) protects against indecency and dishonorable acts.

"Recite what has been revealed to thee of the Book, and establish the prayer; prayer forbids indecency and dishonor. Remembrance of Allah is greater, and God knows what you work on." (Q Ankaboot 45)

Salat Journey:

Salat is the process of establishing a connection that occurs only in a properly prepared setting. Farmers plant the right seeds in suitable soil during the appropriate season to yield a fruitful harvest. Although sowing may seem complete, farmers ultimately depend on the arrival of rain. Thus, the process of farming follows a carefully scheduled journey or itinerary. Sowing is influenced by the farmers' efforts and the impact of rainfall.

In reality, the critical requirement for fruit to grow is rain:

"Have you seen what you cultivate? Is it you who sows, or are We the sowers? If We will, We can turn it into rubble; then you will lament." (*Q* Waqe'a 63)

Rain has the potential to nurture fruit and trees in any location; however, farming aims to ensure that certain fruits are available locally. The Quran makes it clear that Allah wisely controls the rain. He governs the movements of wind and clouds, and can send rain that may be catastrophic to the fruit's crop.

"Have you seen the water that you drink? Are you sending it down from the clouds, or are We the senders? If We will, We can make it bitter. So why are you not thankful?" (Q Waqe'a 64)

Connection is the fruit of salat (prayer). Performing salat prepares the human spirit to receive the rain of mercy through a step-by-step process. When this preparation is complete, the human spirit becomes a place of submission or prostration, akin to a mosque. In this state, the senses yield to the heart, and the humble servant's heart submits and prostrates to the divine essence. Only then can we claim to have established the connection of salat. (Iqamat *Salat*)

This connection requires evidence in the form of divine presence. Experiencing this divine presence allows individuals to find themselves on the "witnessing carpet." Some people may enjoy learning about God through seeing, feeling, traveling, or hearing. When all these experiences intertwine simultaneously, a brief shock may occur, leading the individual to sense the non-existence of their being. In that moment, they realize that the body, senses, and mind are illusory expressions of divine reality.

An important question arises: If the divine breath is one and represented by the Muhammadian primordial reality, why are people different?

While reality is singular, the elements that shape it display countless differences. Everything is created using scaled measures, which rely on water, soil, fire, and air elements. Additionally, human and cultural factors continue to influence these elements.

Process of Creation and Recalling of Self-Clones:

Humankind constantly creates and recalls what it creates. These self-generated images, given life through human breath, reside in high and low stations and can be recalled when the human image matches the recalled image or images.

"This Book of Ours speaks about you in truth. We were transcribing what you used to do" (Q Jathiya 29)

These breath-created self-cloned images are either devilish darkness, thriving on heat-generating sins, or angelic light, thriving on serenity and the coolness of good deeds.

Breath can create angelic or devilish entities. These beings possess illuminating light breath or dark, smoky fire breath. Consequently, recalling them is linked to either an enlightening connection or thick layers of dark veils that enhance disconnection.

Not only that, but with every human breath, each person adds a creation to their spiritual orbit. The other day, after spending the night in the tomb, these created creatures became his own qualified family (Ahl.) This person will return to the doomed family he created, hiding his 'disconnection book' behind his back while calling for his own and their destruction.

These creatures influence the primary reality within us by adding an impact of their breath as a layer of smoky fire surrounds the human heart. They continuously influence the person, being recalled by evil deeds and subsequently rejecting the descent of the rain of mercy. The pure seed would be distant from the heart's soil.

"But as for him who is given his book behind his back, he will call for destruction and enter a Blaze. He used to be happy with his family. He thought he would not return." (Q Inshiqaq 10-14)

On the other hand, good breath movements filled with remembrance and invocation create beautiful creatures that assist in uncovering the pure seed, gaining the reward of connection, and planting further seeds in the spiritual orbit. These will become visualized after death as gardens and rivers. These creatures become the invocator's family, and he will return to them smiling and happy, showing them his book of connection with his right hand.

"As for him who is given his book in his right hand, he will be reckoned with an easy reckoning and will return to his family delighted" (Q Inshiqaq 7-9)

Historical Salat Narrative:

Salat is physically performed only after:

- **Call for Prayer (Azan):** A loud declaration of the call for prayer.

- **A Brief Pause:** During this pause, cleansing, abolition, invocation, asking, or non-obligatory salat performance can be conducted. The rules are not explicitly defined during this phase and are left to general knowledge and accepted norms.

- Second Call for Prayer (*Iqamat*): This is a brief call for immediate gathering and lining up. It is almost half the length of the first call and is called Iqamat *Salat*. Interestingly, and not surprisingly, Iqamat *Salat* means the call to establish prayer.

- The Physical Performance: The act is performed in repetitive units. Body movements are accompanied by recitations from the Quran and specific quotes uttered by Prophet Mohammad, and the performance is finished with a speech called 'Tashahud.'

- The Pre-Salutation Speech (*Tashahud*): Derived from the Arabic word *Shahada* (testimony), *Tashahud* means "trying one's best to testify." Its purpose is to ask Allah to bestow His *salat* (or, once again, endlessly establish His connection) upon Prophet Mohammad (P.B.U.H.) and his family, just as *salat* and blessings were bestowed upon Prophet Ibrahim and his family.

The Historical Journey Itinerary:

Lordship's educational style emphasizes the gradual expansion of concepts over time. Allah conveyed the significance of *salat* through the narrative of humankind.

Disconnection of Humankind: According to human history, the salat (prayer) journey began with Adam and Eve's disconnection from the divinely bestowed presence. They and their descendants had to reestablish this connection step by step through the stories of numerous prophets.

1. **The Call for Connection and the Salat Event (Azan):** This concept is represented by Allah's forgiveness of Adam and

46

Eve, allowing them to return to Him. The verse "Adam received from his Lord's words, so He allowed him to return" implies that the words Adam received are akin to the call for prayer or Azan. The Arabic word Azan originates from a linguistic root meaning "permission."

2. **The Pause Before the Second, Shorter Call for Iqamat Salat (Establishing Prayer):** This phase reflects the years of the pre-Ibrahmic era. The wudu (ablution) is explicitly linked to Noah's flood during this interim pause. Like the wudu, this period serves as an earthly cleansing, preparing individuals to move on to the next stage of their salat journey.

"So We opened the gates of heaven with water pouring down" (*Q* Qamar 11)

3. **The Second Call for Iqamat *Salat*:** This is a milestone for humankind. Ibrahim and his son Ismaeel built the foundation of the House of the Lord in Makkah:

"As Abraham raises the foundations of the House, together with Ishmael, Our Lord, accept from us; You are the Hearer, the Knower" (*Q* Baqaraa 127)

Prophet Ibrahim first made the call for humanity to establish a connection with God. This event marks a significant milestone in the spiritual journey of Adam's descendants as they progress along their path of prayer:

"And call the people to the pilgrimage. They will come to you on foot and every transport. They will come from every distant point." (*Q* Hajj 27)

4. **Perfecting the Salat (The Muhammadian Phase):** This phase focuses on perfecting and completing the *salat*, representing the journey's final milestone.

5. **The Conclusion of Salat (Tashahud):** This final statement captures the words uttered before concluding the performance. Tashahud represents another dimension of *salat*, defining its ultimate goal and objective. This concept was extensively studied on personal, historical, and geographical levels. The *Tashahud* statement quotes:

"Allāh, send prayers upon Muhammad and the family of Muhammad just as You sent prayers upon Ibrahim and the family of Ibrahim."

The Tashahud encapsulates the journey and ultimate objective of the physical performance of *salat*, reflecting a historical demonstration across successive generations of humanity. During the time of Prophet Muhammad, the world reached a pivotal stage of maturity, enabling the perfect establishment of a divine connection.

The numerous disclosures regarding the establishment of the link

Terms	External act	Historical Salat	Spiritual navigation	Internal illumination	Daily routine
First Azan	Call for gathering	Adamic descent to Earth	Internal call for divine knowledge and understanding	Darkness	Night meditation
Pause	During the break, it's time for questions, water purification, and a cleansing ritual.	Noah's people cleansing, flooding	Internal self-cleansing with good deeds and meditations	Darkness and flesh work	
Second Azan (Iqanat)	Call to establish prayer	Ibrahamic phase and building the Kaaba	Meeting an authentic guru and an alternative shining and setting of the divine light	Intermittent Internal illumination	
Takbeer	Initiation slogan	Muhammadian era	Light upon light	Various illumination phases	
Kneeling (Rukoo')	Bending forward	Muhammadian era			
Prostration (Sujoood)	Head on the ground	Muhammadian era			
Witnessing statement (Tashahud)	Declaration of witnessing and asking for a connecting link with the Prophet Muhammad and the Prophet Ibrahim's family	Prophet Muhammad's household's phase	Recall or persistence of the divine light without setting	Persistent self-illumination	
Salutation and exit	Returning to everyday activities as usual	End of time on day one	Servicing people	Telling others about the beauty of the Divine light	Daytime serving people

Figure 5: Multifaceted interpretation of Salat

Encapsulated Facts:

- Prophet Muhammad and his family embody the human aspect of the *salat* concept, linking lordship to servanthood.

- Salat was not mandated as an obligatory ritual until the reality and truth of *salat* became embodied in a person walking among humankind. Allah is fair and capable.

- The human phase of the Lord's command descent precedes the literal revelation of the Gnostic truth.

- Prophet Muhammad and his family represent the humanized *salat* as the embodied connection image, while Prophet Ibrahim and his family exemplify the call to establish *salat*, creating the divine link between the Lord and His servants.

What is the reward for establishing a connection with God?

The rewards are many. The most general and guaranteed reward is gnosis. These heavens of gnosis (Jannat Ma'aref) on earth are trace images or shadows of the heavens of the other day described in the Quran. There are additional rewards based on God's will to whomever He wishes. The last ones are called the gifts of generosity (Karamat). Similarly, these gifts of generosity are traces of higher rewards on the other day after.

How is the gnosis heaven described in the Quran? How can you translate the Quran's verses into your daily spiritual wayfaring routine? How do we break the code of Quranic terminology?

This requires a conceptualization of the descending pattern of the divine commands from meaning to a dual spiritual creation of angels and devils, heavens' ascending stairs and uphills, and hell's downward stairs and pit-holes, and finally into first earth gardens, lavas, and volcanoes, and lower sky with beautiful planets and comets, then finally to scripted letters.

One should be able to ascend from scripture to an imagery knowledge of the lower sky and the Adamic earth we live on, to the heavens and hell. Therefore, gardens become divine gnostic fields; fruit is knowledge and understanding, and rain is mercy and livelihood. Similarly, darkness is ignorance, flames are unlawful desires, and sins are fire. Furthermore, sowing and sowers are the remembrances and the people of remembrance, while the people who bury the seed to hide them from being known are the truth hiders; the plant is a divine disclosure (Tajelliyat). The fertile ovum (Notfa) is the implanted light by the ally (Waliy), the hanging drop (Alaqa) is a stage of the pure growing phase, and the toddler is the child of meaning (Teflul-many). The list is endless.

Acquiring divine gnostic knowledge is not usually didactic. On the contrary, it is demonstrative. For example, to teach a child what a cylinder is, we can give it a descriptive definition of a cylinder. However, if a teacher shows a rectangle that folds until its ends meet to form a cylinder and lets the student feel how a solid cylinder feels, and come up with the definition on their own, the latter educational style results in core understanding and long-lasting comprehension of the essence of the cylinder. Furthermore, teachers can dig deeper and unfold the cylinder before the student's eyes to form two circles and a rectangle and keep redoing the process until fully understood. Eventually, one of the students might realize the cylinder is a line repetition and may argue that the cylinder's reality is just repetitive lines. Another student may argue that a line is a dot repetition, so they have their own taste of knowledge. A third argument may be that a cylinder could be expressed in a formula calculating surface area. The cylinder's shape and numerical expression are different aspects of the same entity. Numbers might have preceded lines in the evolution of the cylinder shape. Then the teacher intervenes and concludes with an open-ended query: since solids are collections of shapes, shapes are repetitions of lines, and lines (or numbers) are repetitions of dots, and dots are similar, could a cylinder be an illusion? Could the cylinder you felt and saw be an imaginary illusion of lines (or digit 1)? Could the digit 1, with its repetitions and its loops, shapes, and solids, be mere expressions of the dot? Could all these diverse creations and constructs be simply the dot trying to define itself?

A student may shout, "So the diversities and differences among creations, and we, the students, are teaching the differences in ourselves to meet every student's understanding levels." The same student rephrases and sums up with a pearl of wisdom: "A dot teaching its diverse manifestations by solidifying shapes and personalizing solids." The teacher quotes: lesson learned. "Existence is to the dot, and we are nothing but traces of illusions." This learning process has a taste to it. This rich conversation and dialogue between this group of students who have tasted knowledge under an authentic teacher will never be comprehended by the group who learned by only defining the cylinder. The defined-taught group may mock, reject, or defy the group that has tasted knowledge, to avoid corrupting the science of cylinder principles. It may even consider them enemies or traitors to the cause of education and demonize them to recruit more followers. This is analogous to the historical heresy or innovation (Bedaa) accusations directed toward illuminated people of God.

The Footsteps of the DOT.

The dot has revealed itself in various forms, changing its appearance by donning different robes or hats. As a result, its manifestations are countless and continually replenished. Allah established a counting system that categorizes these countless manifestations into countable groups of 99, 7, and 3. The lower the number that a spiritual seeker understands, the greater their comprehension. Moreover, the more one experiences, the more gnostic one becomes.

The Trinity concept has been the most widely recognized from a Christian perspective throughout human history. However, the term we will use here is the "Dot Triad," which differs from the Trinity.

The DOT TRIAD:

The *Salat*, or the connection to God, serves as a link. This link can be visualized as the middle hat worn by a dot, connecting the seeker-dot to the manifestations of the seek-to-dot.

This framework also has various triads, including servanthood, lordship, divinity, message, alliance, and prophethood, as well as the divine self, spirit, and divine essence.

For instance, exploring the lordship dot leads to the lordship command, spirit, and thinghood triad. Furthermore, as a manifestation of a dot, the lordship spirit comprises the triad of the word, transcending spirit, immigrant spirit (Hajeer), and a human-like being.

In the thematic world of shapes, any three dots form a straight line or a triangle. Therefore, the thematic world of shapes comprises a vast web of interconnected triangles. In contrast, the world of lines is characterized by countless repetitive lines, while the world of numbers comprises numerous ones.

Humans have reflected this world in their beliefs and religions. The most prevalent concepts are the deviation from the triad to the holy trinity, the shift from replication (Takathor) towards multiplication, and the transition from dot manifestation to the claims of lordship or divinity.

In addition, within the thematic framework of servanthood, a triad parallels similar concepts. Surat Waqea divides this servanthood triad into three distinct parts. When considering the path as a straight line of ascending hypotheses, the top point corresponds to the forerunners (Sabeqoon). The forerunners create a trajectory that starts at this top point and tapers down to a smaller number near the middle point of the straight line.

The middle point corresponds to the people of correct knowledge (Ashabul-*Maimana*). This group forms a rectangular-like trail that maintains its shape and number, extending from the middle point to the lower point manifestation. The Surah refers to another group representing a corrupt counterpart to the righteous people. This group is called the people of wickedness (*Ashabul-Masha'ama*). This latter group signifies a disconnection (Fasl) or represents those who lack prayer (*Salat*) and spiritual connection.

Chapter 6
"The Enlightened Self"

Allah created everything in pairs. So, what is the human pair? Experimental science demonstrates pairing chromosomes from an initial chromatid and their replication. This establishes that every pair has an original image and a replica. On the one hand, we have an external talking, walking, eating, mating, thinking, seeing, hearing, and feeling externally manifesting entity.

On the other hand, we have another entity that has the same attributes but manifests differently. But the perplexing question is, who is the original form, and who is the replica? Are there other copies and replicates? Since every pair is pairable, is this pairing process presumptively endless or not?

As the pairing process continues, defective pairs might evolve. The other end of the pairing spectrum will end with a strain incapable of pairing. Understanding this process logically leads us to have different perspectives, not only of the originality of human beings, the primordial pure self, and the dead-end impurity at the end of the spectrum, but also will help us understand the primordial light, the pure essence (Fitra), the Muhammadian light, or the messenger within ourselves, and the demonic nature of the external entity and its shades of evil.

We can envision a model of three entities: a hidden pure one, a hidden impure one, and the dual apparent entity that can be either, or both. This apparent entity is the external being. The external being is like an apple-shaped fruit that both trees could nurture. Throughout their journey, divine seekers try to search and feed from the pure tree, eliminating the impurity and venom they acquire from the impure tree, or changing from the apple-like double appearance to a fig-fruit-like uniform shape.

During invocation under the guidance of an authentic Sheikh, the seeker begins to perceive his illuminated original form through a series of visions. This manifestation primarily consists of light, shining like stars, the moon, the sun, or as "light upon light." In this experience, he understands that this fist of light form represents his true self. At the same time, all external tools he possesses are merely expressions of the actions of this illuminated self. He then realizes that he is nothing more than a fleeting, fallible shadow of this original reality.

But how can this original reality see, feel, and hear?

The pure original reality sees without restriction (all eyes), hears without limitations (all ears), feels with all hands, and moves spacelessly. Thoughts are seen as knowledge, and creation occurs by command. The sustenance of this reality is invocation; its fruits are revelations. Heaven is gnostic knowledge, while hell represents the consuming fire of love. The byproduct of this process is mercy, and fingerprints signify the divine command descending through moon stations.

It's night is the gnosis of lordship, and daylight signifies the vanishing (Fana) into the divine essence. The star houses are likened to a divine book, with the stars serving as letters. This primordial light acts like a hidden laboratory, manifesting through its externally shadowed entity's merciful, beautiful, and kind actions and behaviors.

Creating harmony between their external surroundings, coupled with the reflection of their inner reality, is extremely essential for external beings to reconnect with their true inner essence. This alignment is most effectively achieved during the tranquil hours of the last third of the night, when the world is quiet and the mind is calm, providing a perfect backdrop for introspection and transformation. The seeker should embark on a journey to learn about lordship through the night journey. They should engage in invoking and counting with their fingers, symbolizing and clearing their moon stations.

Additionally, they must read verses from the Quran to gain insight into the digital book (Marqoom) or the hidden original book (Maknoon). During this journey, the seeker should be visually guided by divine light. This process should continue until sunrise. If the seeker perceives the original divine form during this practice, they are considered connected. If not, they are still an aspiring seeker and should strive harder by increasing their good deeds and actions.

The seeker's night journey begins in the last third of the night. It is the journey of discovering one's true self, not through thinking, comprehension, and imagination, but through valid experiences based on experimentation and observation.

Every experiment consists of inputs, conditions, a process, and a supervising expert that leads to an outcome. The inputs and conditions involve a self-purified seeker, aiming to find the source of purity and manifesting elements from their physical world as a bridge to deeper meanings. This experiment occurs during the last third of the night, when the seeker embraces personal darkness, serenity, and tranquility, serving as a gateway to the unseen reality. The seeker prepares their environment by cleansing themselves and focusing on the lowest point of the sky visible to them. They sit, facing the center of their faith, honored as the pole of Salat (prayer), symbolizing a connection.

They shut down all tangible senses by closing their eyes to look within, searching for the message of God. As they reflect, they realize that every message requires a messenger and understand that Allah is fair, having provided each human being with a guiding messenger. However, this realization comes late in their spiritual journey and only after numerous repeated experiences. As they continue their exploration, the seeker ultimately discovers essential truths in the initial stages of their navigation. They discover that they have a universe within themselves. They see their sky filled with stars and planets. Like a sailor in the dark, they spot the guiding northern star, the first sign of the path to their true self. They begin to navigate toward this guiding star and explore their inner sky. As they continue on this journey, their moon appears. If they persist in their quest until the sunrise of their external world, the sun of knowledge may dawn within. These elements represent the initial stages of a profound journey toward self-discovery, highlighting the notion that deep introspection can reveal secrets that transcend the limits of the human mind. Until this point, while the seeker has begun to forge connections with their inner self, they still find themselves on the periphery of true unity and the whole experience of their illuminated essence.

The seeker may experience moments of clarity and insight that offer a fleeting glimpse of their origin. This could manifest as the perception of a small niche containing a glowing lamp, symbolizing the inner light of awareness. The seeker might also notice the beautiful stained glass colors surrounding the lamp, representing the diverse aspects of their personality and experiences.

In some cases, the seeker may visualize an entire structure as a luminous planet, radiating warmth and wisdom and embodying the interconnectedness of all existence. There may be moments of divine guidance, where unseen forces lead them toward a greater understanding, allowing them to witness a radiant fist of light—an embodiment of strength and clarity that empowers them on their journey. Above all, they might feel overwhelmed by a cascade of light upon light, symbolizing profound revelations illuminating the pathways toward enlightenment and deeper self-awareness.

Allah has created this illuminated self as an intermediary between His absoluteness and the limited nature of His creatures. This self acts as a messenger from God to all creation. It serves various roles: a guide, a witness, a bearer of good news, a warning of bad news, a comprehensive embodiment of the Quran and all scriptures, and a reservoir of what has been, what is, and what will come. It acts as a magnet directing us toward the path to Allah and is described as an illuminated sun (Siraj Muneer). Human beings possess the unique ability to articulate this light and its significant role due to their linguistic, emotional, and rational expressive capabilities.

Throughout history, any divine reality of great significance has been represented by a human being who embodies that reality. This illuminated self-reality has been gradually revealed by pure guides known as prophets and messengers. This progressive revelation, manifested in human form, reached a significant peak with Jesus, who embodied the essence of a soulful human being. However, the ultimate climax is found in the Prophet Muhammad, who represents the ultimate complete reality. He was a humble orphan raised in a deserted environment surrounded by a pagan culture.

Allah selected and chose a specific genetic lineage to be protected from any impurity. These families are mentioned clearly in the Quran: Shieth, son of Adam; Noah; Isaac's family of Abraham; the son of Isaac, Jacob; and the family of Imran, mother of Moses and Aaron. Ismael's descendants quietly paralleled the lineage of Isaac's offspring. Once Jesus was lifted from our domain with no successor, the remarkable appearance of the complete reality was sent to people, and that is the Prophet Muhammad (Peace be upon him and his family and all the prophets).

It is a logical belief that divine revelations will persist until the Day of Judgment. However, many individuals mistakenly assume that Allah has closed the door to sending new messengers to guide humanity. In truth, the narrative unfolds cyclically, with the legacy of spiritual purity entrusted to chosen descendants from the family of the Prophet Muhammad (Al Aitra). Imam Ali and Sayeda Fatima laid the foundation for a lineage of greatness, mainly through their noble offspring, Sayedona Alhassan, the first torchbearers of this sacred light. Each of these descendants embodies a fragment of that collective luminescence, radiating enlightenment and wisdom to the people of their respective eras.

In the authentic traditions of Sunnah, the right hand conveys the notion of authority and is often seen as a symbol of allegiance. This is significant, as these pure descendants of the Prophet Muhammad's family are honored as "Allah's right hand on earth." For those seeking to tread the path of Divine knowledge, offering their pledge of loyalty and recognition to them is imperative, acknowledging their invaluable role in guiding the faithful toward spiritual understanding and enlightenment.

Allah promised to send a messenger to every community: *"And for every Ummah (community or nation), there is a Messenger."* *(Quran, Yones 47)*

Also, in Surah Nahl: "We surely sent a messenger to every community, saying, 'Worship Allah and shun false gods.' But Allah guided some of them, while others were destined to stray. So travel throughout the land and see the fate of the deniers." (Q Nahl 36)

It is a common belief that divine revelations will persist until the Day of Judgment. However, many individuals mistakenly assume that Allah has closed the door to sending new messengers to guide humanity. In truth, the narrative unfolds cyclically, with the legacy of spiritual purity entrusted to chosen descendants from the family of the Prophet Muhammad, known as Al Aitra.

Imam Ali and Sayeda Fatima laid the foundation for a lineage of greatness, mainly through their noble offspring, Sayedona Alhassan, the first torchbearers of this sacred light. Each of these descendants embodies a fragment of that collective luminescence, radiating enlightenment and wisdom to the people of their respective eras.

Allah's rules apply to communities both historically and individually. The principles and regulations set forth by Allah are relevant not only to collective societies and communities throughout history but also to individuals on a personal level. This means Allah's moral and ethical guidelines govern the behavior and actions of both groups and single individuals, shaping their conduct by divine teachings across different contexts and times. Consequently, this leads to a better understanding that Allah created a messenger for each individual. So not only do individuals comprise nations, but also a nation's essence could be collectively gathered into a single individual; *"Indeed, Abraham was a nation (community), devoutly obedient to Allah"* (Q Nahl 120)

This extraordinary human being is far more than just a collection of flesh and bones; he embodies a vast universe that transcends the boundaries of what he can perceive or experience with his limited senses. He represents the spirit of his time and carries within him a unique guiding messenger: *"There has certainly come to you a Messenger from among yourselves. Grievous to him is what you suffer; [he is] concerned over you and to the believers is kind and merciful"* (*Q At-Tawba 128*) Within this lie winding roads, fertile earth, towering mountains, and expansive heavens, all waiting to be explored.

He faces a profound choice: to open his eyes to the distractions of the external world, losing himself in the vivid images that serve only as superficial postcards of life, or to embark on an inward journey, seeking the accurate compass of his existence. By turning inward, he can uncover deep wisdom and establish a path that brings him closer to the divine.

As the spiritual wanderer navigates this inner landscape, he can discover luminous landmarks and signposts illuminating his way. These beacons of insight can be named and described, drawing from his experiences in his physical surroundings, which, while seemingly real, often represent only an illusion. Thus, he can transform his understanding of the world and his place in it, ultimately guiding him back to a profound connection with the divine.

Recap and clarification:

Up to this point, I use equivalent terms such as wanderer, wayfarer, and truth seeker to refer to someone who is in search of divine knowledge to answer common existential questions about where we come from, where we are going, why we were created, and how we came to be. While I have tried to use gender-neutral terms, I occasionally use "he" in a masculine form for simplicity, which can apply to all genders. Additionally, I use the abbreviation PBUH/HF to represent "Peace Be Upon Him and His Family" for greater sensitivity and appropriateness.

I hope that by the end of this book, I will have successfully explained that the seeker's spiritual journey is both internal and visible. During this path, the seeker sees with their heart's eye the stages of returning to their luminous origin of light. They observe their surroundings and try to use what they have learned and named in their transient, illusionary environment to describe these stages of return. They refer to the return as the "path," the initial forms and solid objects as "worlds," an illuminated glimpse of guidance as a "star," the first veil of tangible things and non-tangible thoughts as "darkness," and the dispersion of guidance amidst this darkness as "stars," and so on.

The seekers will understand the intimacy of the divine and the honor of having a personalized, on-demand messenger from within themselves.

As the return process becomes more imminent, the face of the luminous origin is gradually unveiled. The seeker will refer to this transformation as becoming a moon, then a sun (lamp), and ultimately light upon light.

The seeker will understand that prophets (Anbiyaa) and the concept of prophethood are intended for those who share the great news (al-naba' al-'aẓīm) with others. Messengers and their messages, on the other hand, are meant to convey them to their communities.

They will also realize that the visible world around them consists of countless interconnected realms. Their external senses and internal physical structure, created from clay, serve as fragile magnifying lenses, initiating the journey of knowing God—from the micro, through dispersion, to the macro, where everything comes together. Only then can they truly experience unification (Tawheed).

Ultimately, let's suppose the seeker undergoes the shock of divine realization (Saeqa) or the passing phase of awareness (Fanaa). In that case, they will come to know that Allah was, is, and always will be and that there is nothing that exists alongside Him.

May Allah strengthen our connection with our master Muhammad and his family, just as He did with our master Ibrahim and his family. May Allah bless our master Muhammad and his family as He has blessed our master Ibrahim and his family.

Chapter 7

"The Disclosure of the Lordship Roadmap"

People naturally assume names have meanings and backgrounds, and when they encounter an unfamiliar name, they often ask or ponder its significance.

Have you ever wondered what the name "Allah" signifies? What does the inscription of "Allah's name" represent? In today's culture of abbreviated communication, is it acceptable to acknowledge that Allah's name can also serve as a means of conveying hidden or revealed knowledge?

What do the symbolic and graphical elements of the Divine name's letters represent?

The standard definition of Allah is "the majestic name that signifies the essence." However, this definition raises a series of subsequent inquiries.

Next I will try to illustrate the roadmap of Prophecy, Sainthood (Wilaya), and the message, paying special attention to the intricate concept of sainthood or 'wilaya', and differentiating the absoluteness and abstract into creation through the lens of Wilaya, using the analogy of rainbow dispersion from a colorless light beam with the refracting power of a prism.

The Prophecy, Sainthood (Wilaya), and the Message

Passing the news about _Allah revealing His beauty and majesty_ is excellent news (Naba Azeem), and one should hear from those who can witness and validate it.

This great news is mentioned in the Quran in Surah 'Naba.'

"About what are they asking one another? About the great news. That over which they are in disagreement. No! They are going to know" (Q Naba 1-4)

The first input of the divine gnosis is the Great News or great prophecy (Naba al-Azeem). The bearer of this great news or prophecy (Naba) is called a prophet. The other aspect of divine gnosis involves translating the term **Naba** into the creation of the heavens and earth.

Thus, on one side, there are the 'prophets' who can unlock the code from the top down through divine selection, and on the other side, there are individuals who depend on the prophets to help them comprehend the gnostic, detailed model of the earth and heaven. Examples of prophets include Jacob, Isaac, Ishmael, Joseph, Yunus, and Hud Saleh.

Thus, the heavens and the earth serve as a message or a universal pictorial book on the horizon; more specialized prophets can convey this cosmic message to people. These are referred to as 'messengers.' Examples of messengers include Abraham, Moses, Jesus, and Muhammad (PBUH).

Between prophecy and the message lies a transformative intermediary reality known as 'Allyhood' (Wilaya), and the individual tasked with this role is referred to as an ally (**Wali**). Examples of embodiments of Wilaya are S. Al-Khidr, Sidi Jilani, Sidi Abu Hassan Shadhili and his descendant spiritual lineage, Sidi Ahmad Alawi (May Allah sanctify their souls), and the contemporary Wali of the 21st century: My Sheikh Sidi Muhammad Faouzi Alkarkari (May Allah sanctify his secret).

Divine gnosis encompasses numerous pathways. The best invocation is by uttering the Divine name 'Allah,' which enables seekers to lift the veil of darkness, allowing them to attain clairvoyance regarding the 'Great News/Prophecy' and to comprehend the message or savor prophecy and Wilaya.

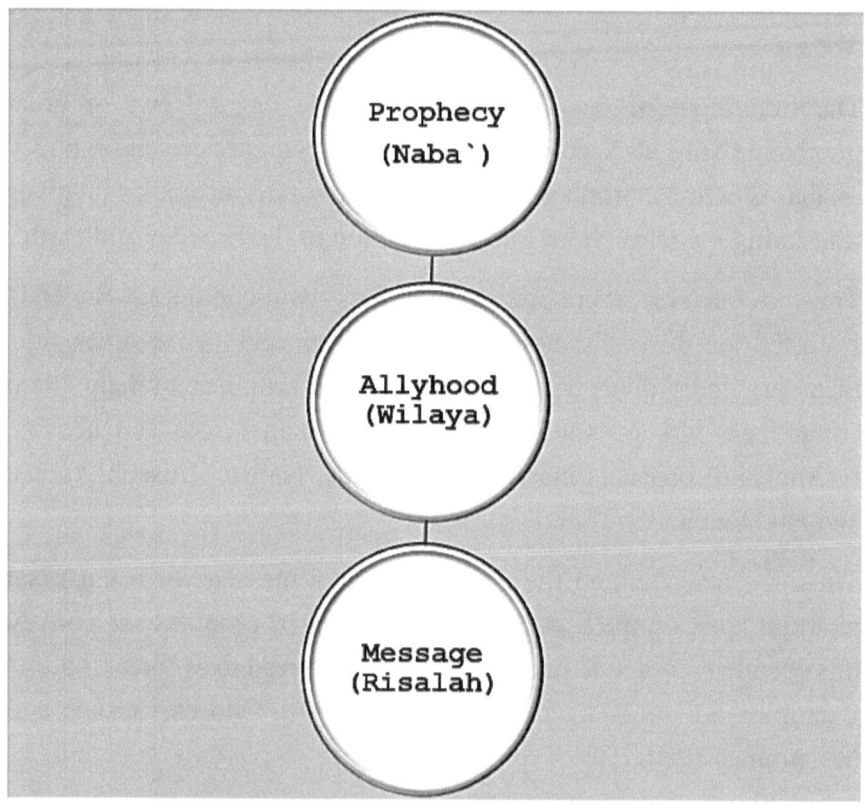

Figure 6: The Lordship Disclosure Roadmap

Creation of Life and Death

The fundamental focus of invocation must be "creation." Most people agree with all theological and non-theological theoretical backgrounds and believe 'things' emerged from 'not a thing' or nothing. Yet they disagree on who or what the igniting force that transformed nothingness into thingness is. Non-theologians hypothesize that something occurred to nothingness; however, this reasoning is not logical because the 'something' that triggers the happening must have existed before nothingness.

A 'nothing' represents death, while 'something' signifies life. The Quran addresses this issue. First, life and death are 'created' entities; second, death precedes life in the creation sequence:

"He Who created Death and Life, that He may try which of you is best in deed" (Q Tabarak 2).

"And is one who was dead and We gave him life and made for him light" (Q Anaam 122).

"And that it is He who causes death and gives life" (Q Najm 44).

Notice the sequence of the words: death followed by life.

'Life' embodies numerous indicators within the realm of possibilities, including movement, action, invention, creation, innovation, oppression, liberation, taking, giving, constriction, expansion, warmth, fire, cooling, water, rain, thunder, love, hate, and light. The aforementioned contrasts with its rival entity, 'death,' characterized by coldness, quietness, silence, stagnation, and darkness. Thus, death is like a tablet or a blackboard that accepts the writing of the Pen of Life to manifest in the world of possibilities.

On the Day of Judgment, Allah will provide a clear understanding of that concept by creating an embodiment of death in the form of a ram. In the Authentic Hadeeth (Sahih Muslim):

"Death would be brought on the Day of Resurrection in the form of a ram. Then, it would be made to stand between Paradise and Hell, and it would be said to the inmates of Paradise: Do you recognize this? They would raise their necks and look towards it and say: Yes, it is death. Then it would be said to the inmates of Hellfire: Do you recognize this? And they would raise their necks and look and say: Yes, it is death. Then, a command would be given to slaughter it. Then it would be said: O inmates of Paradise, there is an everlasting life for you and no death, and then (addressing) the inmates of the Hellfire, it would be said: O inmates of Hellfire, there is an everlasting living for you and no death."

Allah's Messenger (PBUH) then recited this verse, pointing with his hand to this material world:

"Warn them of the Day of dismay when their affairs would be decided, and they would be heedless, and they believe not" (Hadeeth Muslim).

The Sainthood or Allyhood (Wilaya) Conceptualized Reality

An experiment children learn about in school demonstrates that a unified, seemingly colorless beam of light passing through a prism reveals seven distinct, rainbow-like colors. The experiment requires a display area in the space following the prism. This phenomenon is easily observed in nature after heavy rain; the seemingly unicolored sun rays utilize the raindrops as a prism and the horizon as a vast display screen.

Death can be compared to a vacant display screen by connecting the concepts of created beinghood in life and death through the prism of raindrop-induced light dispersion. In contrast, creatures resemble the dispersed particles of light refracting through the prism. The prism or the raindrops serve as a two-sided interface linking the before-individual totality to the after-dispersive multitude of manifestations.

In Sufism, the prism/raindrop analogy signifies the concept of Allyhood, God's friendship, or sainthood, which in Arabic is termed Wilaya. Wilaya is synonymous with the source of life. The human embodiment of the prism/raindrop reality is called a **Wali**. Wilaya, or allyhood, is mentioned repeatedly in the Quran:

"Unquestionably, the allies of Allah—there will be no fear concerning them, nor will they grieve" (*Q* Yunus 62).

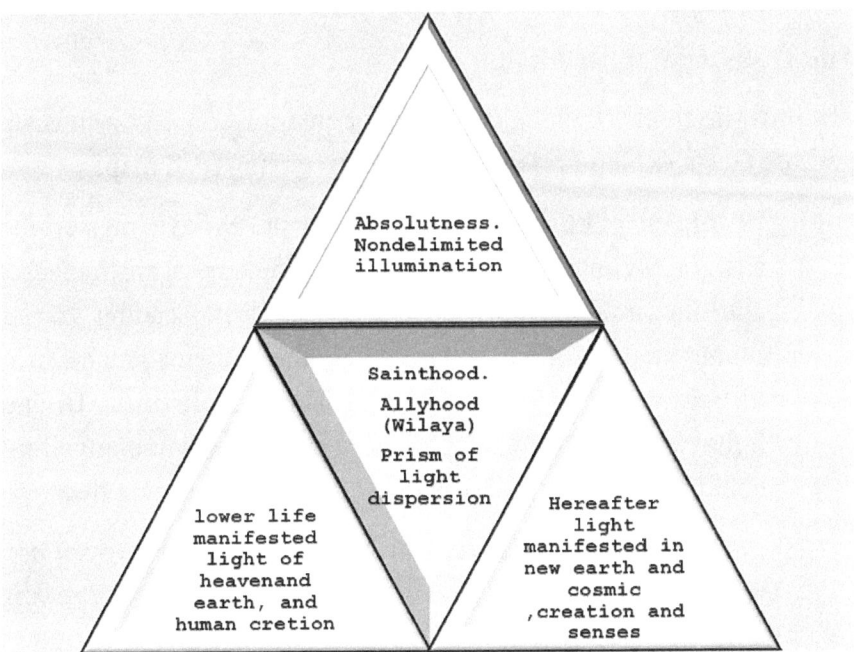

Figure 7: The Centrality of Sainthood in Manifesting and Demanifesting

Belief in **Wilaya** is a fundamental concept in the Quran. Some prophets and messengers also met with the embodied Wilaya of their respective eras. Examples include Al-**Khidr** during the time of Moses:

"And they found a servant from among Our servants to whom We had given mercy from Us and had taught him from Us a [certain] knowledge" (Q Kahf 65); the man with book knowledge during Solomon's time: *" Said one who had knowledge from the Scripture, 'I will bring it to you before your glance returns to you'"* (Q Naml 40); and S. Ali during the time of Prophet Muhammad, **"I am the city of knowledge for which Ali is the door"** (Hadeeth in Tabarani and Mustadrak). Peace be upon them all.

The Transcending Roadmap:

The Sufi wayfarer's theological model of creation consensus consists of three facets, which I refer to as the transcending road map:

1. **Prophecy (The Naba) Phase:** The pre-Wilaya mysterious categories consist of non-delimited absoluteness, abstractness, and the initial reality that can manifest, leading to an illuminated fist of light referred to as the Muhamadian handful of light (Qabdah-Muhammadiya). This sample of the Divine light reflection depicts the great news of the divine unveiling could also be referred to as the 'blessed self-igniting tree'

   "Fueled by a blessed tree, an olive tree, neither eastern nor western. Its oil would almost illuminate, even if no fire has touched it" (Q Nur 35).

2. **Wilaya:** The intermediary source of life, possessing dispersive and collective magnetic power that facilitates life manifestations.

3. **The Message:** The tangible outcome of the Wilaya work expresses the Great News through communicable means. The message descends in tablets, with the highest tablet being the preserved tablet (Lawh Mahfoozh), followed by seven tablets, one for each of the seven heavens. It then moves to the star-sites (Mawaqeal-Nojoom), referring to the secretive hidden tablet (Kitab Maknoon) in the lowest sky. "So I do swear by the positions of the star site. and this, if only you knew, is indeed a great oath ‹that this is truly a noble Quran, in a hidden book" (Q Al-Waqi`ah 75-78)

The Kitab Maknoon in the start site positions further manifest as twinkles of starlight perceived by the eyes and forming a digital book (Kitab Marqoom). "But no! The virtuous are indeed bound for an extremely high location, and what will make you realize what this high location is? a digital book, witnessed by those who are drawn near" (Q Al-Mutaffifeen 18-21).

Finally, it is presented as a tablet written in letters and lines (Kitab Mastoor), referring to the holy scriptures. "By Mount Ṭûr! And by the written Book, on open published pages" (Q At-Tur 1-3).

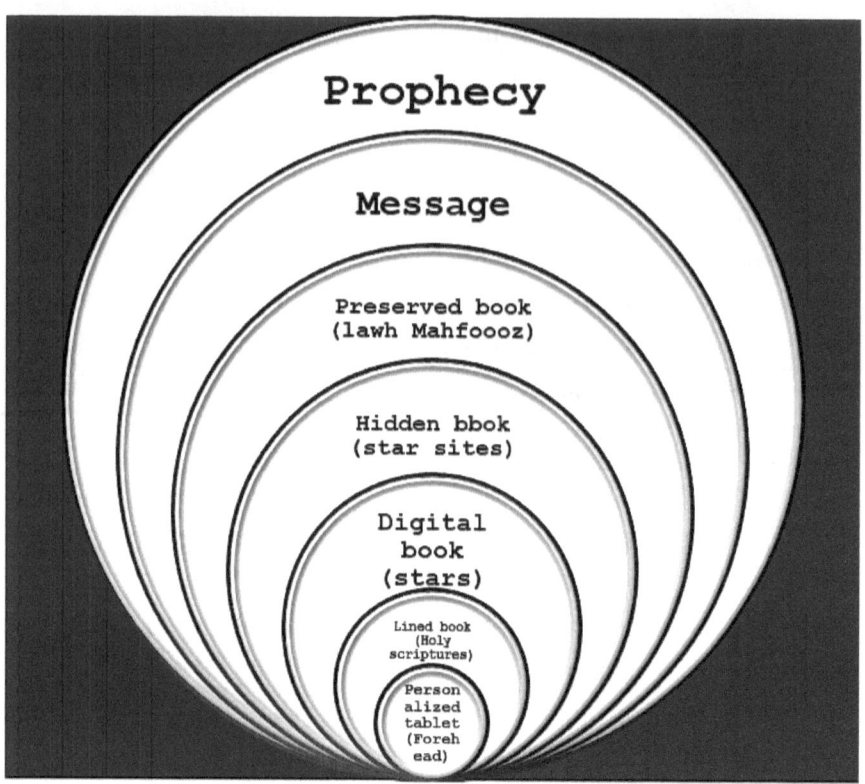

Figure 8: Transitional Phases of Message Revelation

The final transition of the message phase presents and displays letters, numbers, shapes, and solid manifestations of the ultimate reality of the 'Naba' phase. The fanning out of these manifestations indicates that the closer one is to the prism of sainthood, the more consolidated truth presents itself, and the less dispersed and refined one's knowledge of the 'Naba' reality becomes, while the farther one is from the prism, the less gnostic knowledge one acquires.

Additionally, we can envision that the 'lower life' is much farther from the prism of Wilaya than the 'hereafter other life.'

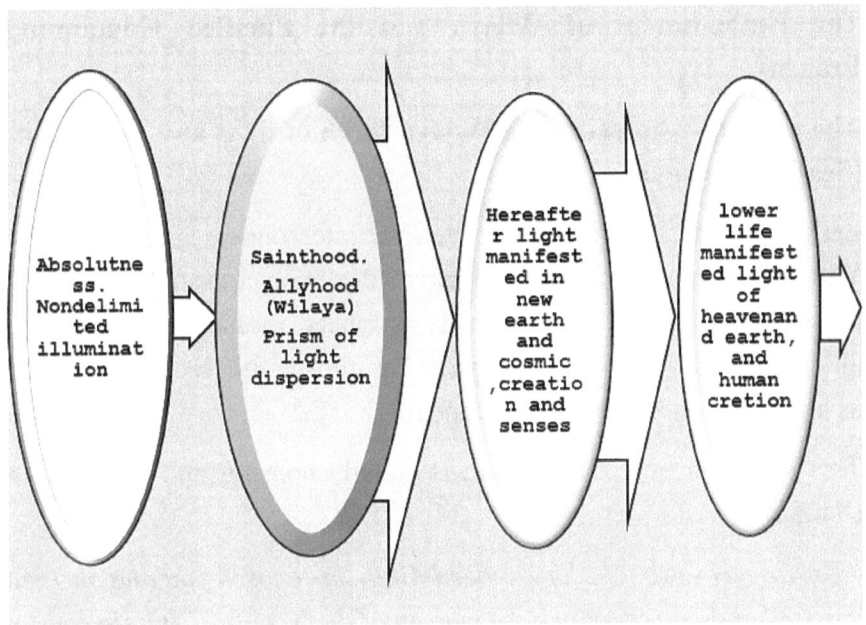

Figure 9: Sainthood's Translational Role from Absoluteness to Possibility Realms.

Therefore, the hereafter life is more definitive and revealing of the 'Naba' than the contemporary lowermost life. For instance, the manifestations of unlawful desires are presented as an inflaming fire in the hereafter. Lying, stealing, backbiting, or fornicating would have opposite expected manifestations compared to those typically associated with a lower level of existence. People will see the reality of good deeds and character as gardens and castles. Even good people will have people they have created themselves, forming families and spouses:

"Indeed, the companions of Paradise, that Day, will be amused in joyful occupation. They and their spouses—in the shade, reclining on adorned couches. For them therein is fruit, and for them is whatever they request" (*Q* Yaseen 55–58).

The Embodiment of Wilaya and the Purified Humankind Progeny

The persons who carry the Wilaya torch of light and the stamps (Seal) of approval.

Let us incorporate a loosely related yet interconnected concept. The Wilaya's most central and inclusive revelation appears in the pure progeny of humankind known as prophets, messengers, or God's allies (**Awliya**). Furthermore, Allah has chosen this sect of humanity as a lineage among family descendants.

This selection process in Islam is called choosing and purification (Istifaa):

"The angels said, 'O Mary, indeed Allah has chosen you and purified you and chosen you above the women of the worlds.'" (Q Ala Emran 42)

This divinely orchestrated top-down purification of a particular lineage serves as a mercy to humankind, as the lineage is acknowledged. It blocks the way for eloquent impostors.

Furthermore, this purification is contagious and can be embraced by all humankind who choose to follow the purifying role models assigned by God. This selection may falsely seem unfair. However, a skeptical person might not mind being selected to be the offspring of the most famous, wealthy, or influential family of their time.

Purity runs in selected families, akin to fame, wealth, influence, or royalty. However, unlike the exclusive and often temporary inheritances of others, purity provides an open and enduring path for anyone who wishes to pursue it:

"Those were the ones upon whom Allah bestowed favor from among the prophets of the descendants of Adam and of those We carried with Noah, and of the descendants of Abraham and Israel, and of those whom We guided and chose. When the verses of the Most Merciful were recited to them, they fell in prostration and weeping" (Q Maryam 58).

"And We granted to him Isaac and Jacob—each/all We guided—and Noah We guided from before, and from his descendants [are] David, and Solomon, and Job, and Joseph, and Moses, and Aaron. And like that, We reward the good doers" (Q Anaam 64).

"And [mention] when the angels said, 'O Mary, indeed Allah has chosen you and purified you and chosen you above the women of the worlds.'" (Q Ala Emran 42).

The Early and Late Post-Wilaya Two-Day Disclosures:

Adam (PBUH), after the earthly descent, was the archetypical late post-Wilaya disclosure in the lowest life. This Adamic reality evolved through history into the more complex revelation of the same reality in Moses and Jesus, ultimately culminating in the collective reality of the Prophet Muhammad (PBUH).

Adam carried with him both the purity of Wilaya, which he transmitted to his son Sheith, and the burden of sin, which he conveyed to his other son, Qabeel. He was an immaculate person inside and out, yet his occupation involved moving dirt from one place to another.

The Wilaya that Adam's son, Sheith, inherited continued through generations, remaining within the family of Noah, then Abraham, and the sons of Israel (Jacob). It later reappeared in the lineage of Ismael and culminated in the Prophet Muhammad and the descendants of S. Fatima, the daughter of the Prophet Muhammad (PBUH).

The disclosure of the Wilaya and its embodiment within the family of Prophet Muhammad becomes more evident as we approach the early post-Wilaya (early message) days of the hereafter. This clarity contrasts with the late post-Wilaya (late message) period during the briefest days of life.

The Chronological Versus Spatial Disclosure of Wilaya: The Higher Companion Reality

Do you know that you have a personal role model within you? This role model is the better version of yourself that you strive for. This highest companion is referred to in this book as 'Hajeer,' and is closer to your original, holy reality. This entity is more authentic than the one you believe is you in life's current, illusory far-reality.

Using the Example of Adam's Earth Compared to Adam's First Heaven Versions:

The story of Adam and the subsequent prophets and messengers to humankind unveils the chronological sequence of the disclosure of the Wilaya reality, contrasting it with the spatial, non-chronological disclosure of Wilaya. The historical chronology of Adam's manifestations in the journey of descent on earth differs from the vertically manifested Adamic reality in the first heaven as disclosed to the Prophet Muhammad (PBUH) during the night journey.

The night journey took place when the Prophet Muhammad was lifted to witness the manifestations of reality within the seven heavens. These manifestations and revelations of distinct realities unfolded in seven separate categorical sequences. In this unveiling journey, the Prophet Muhammad encountered the spirits of the seven prophets in a different sequential order, starting from Adam, followed by Jesus, Joseph, Idris, Aaron, and Moses, and culminating with the most exalted, Abraham. Each prophet corresponds to one of the seven heavens.

The lowest heaven is supported by the Adamic reality, the second by the Christ reality, and so forth until the Abrahamic reality influences the seventh heaven. Thus, on the Day of Judgment, believers will be with those they followed and identified with, becoming a reflection of that reality. This concept is more straightforward if one can distinguish between the human model who walked the earth among these purified figures and the reality they represented.

This dual version applies to Adam and his descendants, providing a magnificent role model to look up to. This 'Highest Companionship' is evident in the authentic hadeeth, wherein the Prophet chose departure over staying on earth, quoting the very popular phrase:

"No, I chose the Upper Companion."

When death approached, his last words were, "O Allah! (with) the highest companion." The Quran hints at the name change when an individual becomes their highest companion. This is shown in the Quran when Jesus mentions the name of the forthcoming prophet, Ahmad, instead of Muhammad:

"And [mention] when Jesus, the son of Mary, said, 'O children of Israel, indeed I am the messenger of Allah to you, confirming what came before me of the Torah and bringing good tidings of a messenger to come after me, whose name is Ahmad.' But when he came to them with clear evidence, they said, 'This is obvious magic'" (Q Saff 6).

Therefore, the upper companionship reality of the Prophet of Islam's name is Ahmad (meaning the most praised or praised), not Muhammad (the excessively praised).

The prism of differentiations, the raindrop, the life generator, or the seal of differentiation is identified in the Sufi concept as the seal or the stamp holder (**Al-Khatem**). One appears every hundred years, as per a known authentic hadeeth with Sufi interpretation.

Chapter 8
"The Disclosure of Lordship in Numbers and Letters"

The transcendence of the letters' journey from the realm of meaning to symbolic scribing. The implications of the interaction between the realms of letters and their subsequent spatial and chronological manifestations on human civilizations, as well as their influence on the establishment of contemporary systems, laws, configurations of the current illusional life, and the prospective, more realistic day of the hereafter.

Tracing this reality back, the book can be distilled into a title that condenses into a precious drop of ink, leading to the realm of meanings in the author's mind, onward to the abstract, and finally to the realm of absoluteness. Readers of a book vary in their levels of comprehension as they progress through different stages of connecting with the text. The more immersed they become, the more captivated they feel. Furthermore, the closer they get to the initial "drop of ink that came from the author's pen," the more they relate to the book's concept.

Book titles concisely represent the book's letters and sentences, reflecting the authors' thoughts. The initial concepts create a realm of meanings, unveiling intangible secrets drawn from the authors' reservoir of knowledge. The first insight that inspired the title was like a precious drop of ink capturing all the book's essential elements.

The Dot Is the Soul of the Letters

'Letters and numbers represent my whole being and perceiving my *continuum,*' the ink Dot, hypothetically, stated:

How have letters come into existence from the world of meaning? What occurs first: letters or numbers? Do letters have reference numbers? What are the primary letters in the order of revelation?

Reflecting on the letter discussion, this journey of letters and numbers spans from infinity to the abstract, from the illuminated fist of light to the first collective ink dot. It also involves objectifying the realms of letters and numbers, the early and late revelation of the alphabet, and the shaping and systematizing of the universal structure based on the relationships and interactions among the realities of letters and numbers.

Assigning a name and a symbol to a letter is similar to naming a galaxy and depicting its form with a mixed circular drawing. The more we grasp this idea, the deeper our understanding of the letter and the more curious we are during our spiritual journeys and explorations. It may surprise us, the inhabitants of lower life, that the letters we trace represent the most fundamental expression of the original letter essence in the 'world of letters' nearest to the 'prism of Wilaya.'

The same concept applies to other numerical realms. Furthermore, we can anticipate that the sequence of alphabetical letters in the lower realms, distant from the prism, differs from that of the afterlife, closer to the source Wilaya.

Letters are created and included in the post-Wilaya's (message) phase. From a Quranic perspective, this message phase of 'life' has two dimensions: the lower life (Hayat **Dunya**) and the hereafter (Hayat **Akhira**). As stated:

"But you prefer the lowermost life, while the Hereafter is better and more lasting" (*Q* Al-Aa'la 16-17).

We can expect that both lives share a similar concept while differing in manifesting the pre-prism reality.

A relatable quote from S. Ali is more referenced in Shia Muslim texts than the Sunni school: "Everything in the Qur'an is in the opening of the book (Al-Fatiha), and everything in Al-Fatiha is in (Bismillah Al-Rahman Al-Raheem), which is the first verse of Al-Fatiha, and everything in the first verse is in the first letter 'Ba,' and everything in 'Ba' is in the dot scribed under the 'Ba,' and I am the dot under the 'Ba."

The Eruption of the Letter Realm:

As I mentioned earlier, the letters we recognize in our Earthly world emerge from a series of different representations on various tablets. Consequently, these written letters represent the manifestation of elevated realities.

Viewing the manifestation of letters differently, letters and numbers were part of the eruption cascade that disclosed the initial reality. This eruption originated from the first fist of light, which manifested as the Pen. The Pen produced its very first dot of ink to write about what was and will be. By viewing creations as replications of this reality in various shapes, forms, consistencies, and densities, we can conclude that letters and numbers are categorical manifestations (Tajilliat) of the precious ink dot, which contains the collectively gathered essence of the Pen, referred to here as the Dot (*Al Nokta*). The Dot is a subtle secret that flows into every creation, manifesting differently.

Imagining that the Dot can converse, it hypothetically states, "I am the deputy of the primordial fist of light. I am the precious first and only drop of ink the Pen produced. My capabilities are limitless. I will continue descending by adding layers of countless shades to transform meaning into tangibility and sensibility. My structure of creation is based on the hierarchical descent of meanings, with each fundamental meaning represented by an individual who embodies a specific level of truth. These individuals will come to know one another through me, and, in essence, my entire self perceives my continuum. It is my reflection on myself as they learn about me. This way, I introduce myself to myself, stemming from an inherited desire to be known." The dot further added, "I am an intermediary between my dispersed continuum and my whole origin."

The concepts of singularity, uniqueness, self-sufficiency, non-fractionability, and the capacity to multiply to form a category of meaning establish a linear realm with a specific name and shape: it is called "One," and its shape is a straight line. The digit '1' in the lowest realm is the essential lowest trace of such reality. As humankind continues to evolve, this numerical realm of knowledge may correspond to a parallel symbolic realm referred to as "Aleph." In this manner, Aleph represents a mirrored manifestation of "One."

Therefore, using shapes and figures, tracing letters in specific sequences, or even uttering certain words at specific counts or frequencies becomes a form of communication with these realms. At times, the intentions behind such communication are malicious, historically known as black magic. Pursuing this type of knowledge is a double-edged sword, and since it is rarely sought for the sake of goodness, all religions have prohibited its teaching purposes. Indeed, some individuals may find these concepts illogical, yet the same people can be easily swayed by a few written, spoken, or heard words that transform their emotions from anger to happiness, leaving them emotionally affected, spiritually uplifted, or driven by carnal desire. Why do such reactions occur in response to simple audible or visible words?

The Letters of the Divine Name 'Allah':

The name in Arabic letters reads (الله) It consists of four letters: Alif (ا) Lam (ل), Lam (ل) and Ha (ه). Viewing the name as a roadmap to its essence, it features four letters and three vacant spaces. Since one of the letters is duplicated—specifically, the 'Lam'—the name comprises only three distinct letters: Alif (ا) Lam (ل), Lam (ل) and Ha (ه).

In the authentic hadeeth: "Allah created the 'Pen' and commanded it to write. The Pen said: What should I write? He said: Write down what was and what will eternally be." (Hadeeth in Termedhi and similarly in Tabarani).

In Arabic calligraphy, the Aleph is represented by a straight line drawn from top to bottom, featuring a single stroke, a tapered lower end, and a slight leftward slant. Each letter has specific measurements for its vertical and horizontal lengths, using a unit called 'Nokta.' In Arabic, 'Nokta' means 'dot.' The Aleph measures seven vertical dots in the commonly used 1/3-based Arabic calligraphy style, Thuluth.

Allah's Name: The Roadmap to Gnosis

Reflecting on Allah's name serves as a roadmap to divine gnosis. Individuals on Sufi paths, particularly those in the Karkariya Sufi Order of the 21st century, begin their gnostic education by studying the last letter from right to left, 'Ha'—equivalent to 'H' in English. They seek to understand the circular 'Ha' manifestation in the world around them and within themselves during the day. They also search for the metaphorical realm of the 'Ha' disclosure during the twice-daily meditative invocation that occurs after sunset and before and immediately after sunrise. During this invocation, they seek to unveil reality and reflect on the creation of heaven and earth by the Quran's instruction:

"Those who remember Allah while standing or sitting and lying on their sides and give thought to the creation of the heavens and the earth, [saying], 'Our Lord, you did not create this aimlessly.'" (*Q* Al-Imran 3:191).

Aleph's Length and Transformation into Lam:

The length scale of the Aleph is equivalent to seven vertical dots. If one cups the lower end of the Aleph and extends its five dots horizontally, it transforms into a Lam. If Aleph humbles itself to manifest as a letter of a closer rank, this letter shape is referred to as Lam.

Thus, if Aleph manifests a second-ranked letter to follow or to be a step down from Aleph's pride while remaining individual and infinite, Aleph will use the veil of being a Lam. In other words, if the Aleph realm transforms into another realm, the latter will possess new qualities, and this new realm will be referred to as a Lam realm/world.

A well-versed Sufi individual may perceive the Lam as a veiled Aleph seeking recognition. Additionally, the Sufi individual might refer to the Lam as *"the* most proximal or greatest veil of the Aleph."* The Aleph behind the Lam's veil is curved and leans towards non-Aleph letters that are defined and could resemble a circle if extended. The Lam is neither a straight line nor a circle. It serves as a deputy (Khalifa) representing the Aleph.

Implications of the Veil of the Lam During Sufi Spiritual Navigation:

It signifies that one can only attain Aleph's knowledge or come close to understanding the Lam Library of Knowledge through the gate of the 'Ha' realm. If one remains skeptical about this knowledge, they will focus on letters, tracing fonts, and cursive rather than on worlds, realms, and knowledge libraries that bring them closer to the divine. Their period on the Day of Hereafter will be more rigorous and prolonged because we are all returning to God, no doubt (*Inna Lillahi wa Inna Ilayhi Raji'un*).

Nevertheless, the opportunity to become a forerunner exists in this lower life, where mercy prevails and ignorance can be erased.

The first letters penned by the Pen are Alif, Lam, and Ha. These correspond to the initial post-Wilaya (early message) phase of the Hereafter era, in contrast to the order of the alphabet during the later post-Wilaya (late message) phase of the contemporary lower-life era, which begins with Aleph, followed by 'Ba,' then 'Jeem,' then 'Dal,' and so forth in the Arabic alphabet. The sequence in which Aleph manifests as 'Ba' has also influenced the structure of the lowermost life system.

The letters Aleph, Lam, and Ha encapsulate the story and represent the early creation phase. Alif signifies absoluteness and the concept of endlessness, extending indefinitely. Lam represents the inevitable curvature of any straight line, suggesting that all paths eventually form a circle in the realm of physical possibilities. Ha, on the other hand, symbolizes a circular delimitation of existence's timeless, spatial nature.

A question that may perplex mathematicians is whether a straight line would become a circle if we assumed the radius of infinity. The answer lies in Allah's name, inscribed in Arabic letters. The answer is yes. Each letter of "Allah" conveys a deeper meaning, reflecting different perspectives. This also illustrates the orbital-shaped and compressed appearance of the cosmos we observe. In Sufi terminology, these orbits represent the disclosures of the Ha.

However, this topic is beyond the scope of this chapter, and I will discuss it in detail in my upcoming book, "The Name."

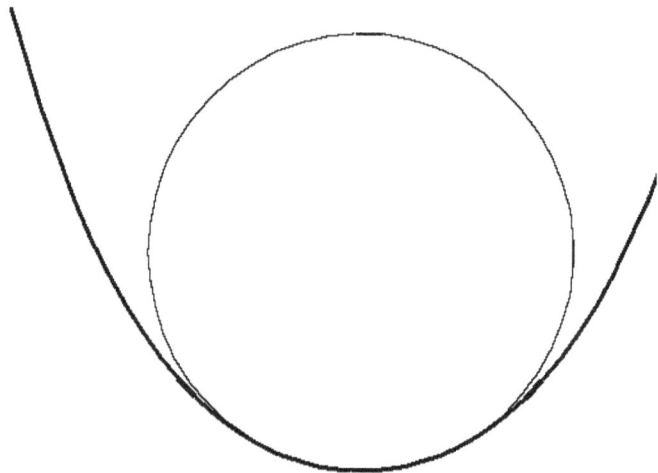

Figure 10: Hypothetical Straight Line if the radius is Infinity

The Fundamental Islamic Slogan:

The fundamental Islamic slogan of no deity but Allah (La *Ilaha Illa Allah*). A careful examination of this phrase reveals the three primary letters of Allah's name in different sequences, allowing the Alif to either precede or follow the Lam or to occur in isolation with a space before and a space after. Furthermore, the Ha is always connected to the Lam, which never appears in isolation and never precedes the Lam. The Lam always precedes the Ha or is supported by the Alif, or it can even appear duplicated as a double Lam.

From a non-Arabic-speaking perspective, one can view the tracing as a single vertical line that could extend infinitely—two vertical lines connected on one side and infinite on the other. Two lines connected horizontally form a circle with a center. Spaces are hidden and imperceptible content.

How Have Meanings Emerged From Complete Abstractness to letter format?

Metaphysically, a circle has no beginning or end; thus, it does not convey the meaning of time but rather represents space. In contrast, time—and, to a lesser extent, space, are depicted on a horizontal line, while a vertical line illustrates transcendence and changes in value. This interplay between the various representations of a line and a circle could shape our understanding of the world.

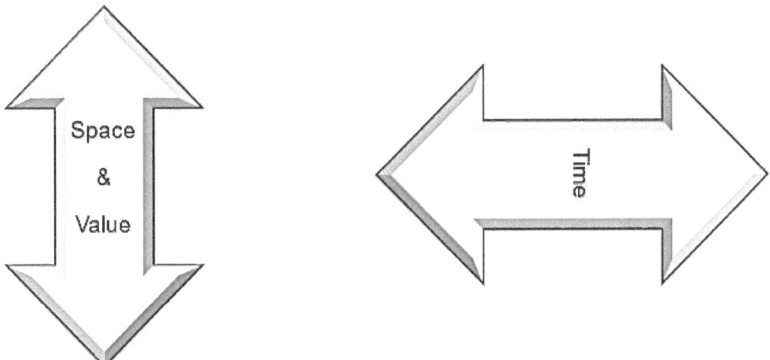

Figure 11: Horizontal and Vertical Depiction of Spatial, Temporal, and Scalable Kartoon of Revelation

Other figures emerge from lines and circles. These intermediary figures reveal the secrets of multiplication and the creation of pointed shapes such as triangles, squares, and hexagons etc. Time, place, and value can be expressed in degrees using measurable angles in these shapes.

Pointed figures can also be considered as transformed circles. They transcend meanings to convey unlimited expressions and signify a crucial master archetype behind the revelations of what makes a straight or circular line pointy: the Dot.

Therefore, without the Dot, no lines, circles, or revelations would exist.

Chapter 9
"Divinity and Parables"

The "As-If you see Him" Image:

Allah (SWT) has no equal, and nothing is like Him; therefore, He created a parable referred to as the "as-if Image." He later created humankind in this as-if image and endowed them with specific qualities and instincts to serve as examples. Islam explicitly prohibits the worship of any "as-if" image, a pitfall into which humanity has repeatedly stumbled throughout history. People have worshipped humans and animals or crafted images and statues, often placing them in areas devoid of "idols."

It is essential to remember that both ancient and modern pagan cultures recognize these images as not God but rather as intermediaries.

This reasoning is a weakened justification for flawed theology, as humans cannot create intermediaries but must rely on those divinely appointed. Trustworthy intermediaries connect God and His creation, acting as God's deputies on earth or as chosen ones appointed directly by God, each with their proof. The first prototypical deputy (Khalifa) on earth was Adam. The angels' prostration marked his appointment, and his proof of deputy-hood was his knowledge of the divine name and his ability to teach the angels what they did not know, by taking them on a reverse journey from the names or word tracings to the named or word reality using the various expressive capabilities Allah endowed in him.

Human Intermediaries and Their Role:

Although human intermediaries encompass the entire "as-if image," each has specific tasks to perform and limits to observe. Some convey news and strive to educate people about uncovering the truth; these are known as prophets. Other intermediaries, or deputies, reveal prophecies through written letters, tablets, newspapers, or books; they are called messengers. Some specialize in guiding individuals from the darkness of ignorance to the light of closeness with the Creator; these are God's friends or allies (Awliyaa).

Allah has given humans experiences to simplify the creation process and to understand what it means to strive for an "as-if image." An author, motivated by a desire for recognition, writes a book. Through his perspective, he reveals beauty worth sharing. He uncovers knowledge he never realized he had, and as he delves deeper, he finds even more, much to his surprise. Some might quote, "suddenly as if a light bulb has turned on," transforming this initial, primordial, intangible thought into a subtle force that drives him to write his book. This light bulb is self-igniting and continues to illuminate pathways in his mind.

Some authors keep the self-igniting light bulb hidden, obscured by self-absorption clouds, or intentionally conceal it. Conversely, an author may choose not to write the book because the end users are unprepared to grasp the novel or require other introductory texts to equip them for adequate comprehension. Other authors may wish to explore pathways of transcendence and use their tools for revelation. These tools—the tongue, teeth, lips, and fingertips—reflect the physical aspect of their mental pathways. The journey from light bulbs to detailed, streamlined ideas raises the question of who oversees this precise, meticulous process. Who performs the micromanagement? What is the intermediary between the light bulb and its final physical expression through the mouth and fingertips?

Allah created the cosmos as a template for authors, non-authors, and humanity to address the question of precise creation. He revealed seven skies and seven earths. He created a sun that appeared in twelve mansions (Burooj) and a moon with thirty stations (Manazel *Qamar*). The result is the rhythmic flow of ocean tides responding to the moon's presence and movement in her stations. This tide-driven motion, guided by the moon, requires the movement of wind and air. As the winds shift, temperatures fluctuate, and rain falls.

Let's imagine that making a change in the physical realm (Mulk) originates from the realm of invincibility (Jabaaroot) before it goes through the spiritually illuminated realm (Malakoot). The divine command of "Be" from this realm of invincibility descends through the seven heavens, revealed by the sun rising in its mansions, the moon moving through her stations, and expressed through the winds, clouds, rain, and tides.

Similarly, just as the universal structure relates to humankind and exemplifies divinity to humanity, the command to "be novel" acts as a subtle force that ignites a self-sustaining light bulb within the invincible mind of humankind. This light moves up and down, guided by a governing torch of illumination—the "mind's moon"—which illuminates pathways of thought. It inspires the winds of counter-argumentative potential along with the rain of ideas that cleanse the ocean of logical thinking from the frothy tide of ambiguity.

The book title resembles a diamond raindrop that falls and transforms into an ink droplet from the pen of revelation. A well-versed, eloquent author crafts the title, using sounds and letters to translate the thoughts of their creatively illuminated mind into written words. They elaborate, explain, provide details, give examples, and describe emotions to effectively depict their genre, conveying the title to the reader. The author's command bursts forth in ecstasy as their most valuable first drop of ink falls upon the fallible tablet from their internal ocean of knowledge. They declare the book title, knowing that this precious, primordial ink drop encapsulates and secretly connects the book to its creator. This ink drop is like the soul of the book.

Recap:

This detailed creation model spans from absoluteness and abstractness, the original luminous fist of light, to the differentiation of the Divine primordial light. This process of differentiation leads to the emergence of things, much like different colors arising from a single collective light passing through a dispersion prism. This creative differentiation of creatures and things requires a prism that imparts their characteristics, stamping them with distinct attributes.

The human embodiments of this seal surface among us every hundred years as a magnetic force that attracts those marked with the seal of goodness. Acting as a reviver of Sufi knowledge, they fulfill the prophetic saying: "Allah sends to my nation a person every hundred years to renovate their *religion*" (Hadeeth). This relationship between the human seal and the sealed entities manifests as a bond between prophets and believers or between a guru (Sheikh) and followers (*Murideen*).

The differentiation process encompasses everything that is not human, including the cosmic structure and the numerous inhabitants we know or do not know. Differentiation begins as numerical realms, representing a multiplication of the "one." These numbers manifest as realms of inscribed lines. The worlds are formed through the interaction of the numerical and scripted letter realms, as illustrated in the latest disclosure tablet. This includes creatures, human and non-human structures, the cosmos, and galaxies.

The Prism that symbolizes the Seal of *Wilaya's* distinguishing power is historically reflected in the tales of the prophets, messengers, and Awliyaa. It also metaphorically appears in the afterlife and in the fundamental rules, laws, and systems of the lower life.

May Allah strengthen our connection with our master Muhammad and his family, just as He did with our master Ibrahim and his family.

May Allah bless our master Muhammad and his family, just as He has blessed our master Ibrahim and his family.

Chapter 10
"The Disclosure of Lordship in Images"

"Allah created Adam in His image" said a hadith (narrated in Bukhari and Muslim). Other authentic narrations quote the hadith as: "Allah created Adam in the image of the Merciful."

How could Adam be in Allah's image or the image of the Merciful? What is the definition of that image? Why is it prohibited in Islam to depict Allah in drawings or create crafted pictorial representations or statues? Does looking at Adam or his descendants teach us who Allah is? Does this imply that Allah has a shape? Why does the Quran clearly state that God has no likeness or comparison?

We must understand the differences between image and comparison, example and likeness, 'as if' and 'literally is,' God's deputyship and God, Divine Allyhood (Wilayah), and Divinity (Uluhiyyah). Understanding these distinctions enables us to recognize the fine line between servanthood and lordship.

The concept of image-hood, God's deputyship, and divine allyhood are all examples of the reality of divinity. Allah taught this in the Quran by providing examples and repeatedly referring to the 'image of His image.'

Using parables as a common Quranic style is demonstrated in numerous verses:

"Give them a parable about this present life. It is like water. We have sent down from the sky, with which the earth's plants mingle and turn

to become dry remnants scattered by the winds. Allah is Powerful over all things." (Q Al-Kahf 18:45)

"And you lived among the dwellings of those who wronged themselves, and it had become clear how We dealt with them. And We presented for you [many] examples." (Q Ibrahim 14:45)

"Allah has struck an example of a man shared by disagreeing partners, and a man who fully agrees with another man. Are the two equally alike? Praise belongs to Allah, but most of them do not know." (Q Az-Zumar 39:29)

The next logical question is: what is the 'image of the image'? What image is created to resemble Adam?

The 'image of the image' serves as an educational tool for understanding the original image. It allows viewers to grasp the concept of imagery and understand that this image is a descriptive vessel shaped to convey meanings of reality. Thus, the image is not the actual reality, just as the 'image of the image of the image' is not the original but a filtered, dispersed representation of the original image's intangible meaning in a visual form.

However, to accurately depict reality, the image must follow the instructions to be a mirror image. The same applies to the 'image of the image.' It must first reflect the original image to be representative of it.

Following this line of reasoning, it becomes apparent that the image of Adam and his descendants represents the 'universe.' Allah created the universe according to specific systems that reflect the Adamic race, assisting them in understanding themselves and, in turn, enabling them to utilize these insights on their journey toward divinity.

Subordination or Submission (Islam) of the universal cosmic image of Adam:

"It is Allah who created the heavens and the earth and sent down rain from the sky and produced thereby some fruits as provision for you and subjected for you the ships to sail through the sea by His command and subjected for you the rivers. And He subjected for you the sun and the moon, continuous [in orbit], and subjected for you the night and the day." (Q Ibrahim 14:32–33)

Since this system serves as an educational interface, it is built on principles of subordination to educate people. Additionally, it includes experimental lab functions, safety measures, and a self-correcting maintenance system to address the learning needs arising from students' mistakes.

"Corruption has appeared throughout the land and sea by what the hands of people have earned, so He may let them taste part of what they have done, that perhaps they will return." (Q Ar-Rum 30:41)

If Utopia existed, it would encompass a subservient universe and compliant beings. This utopia would result from a process of double submission (Islam). *"Certainly, Allah's only Way is [Islam] submission." (Q Aal-E-Imran 3:19)*

"So is it other than the religion of Allah they desire, while to Him have submitted those within the heavens and earth, willingly or by compulsion, and to Him they will be returned?" (Q Aal-E-Imran 3:83).

"And whoever desires other than submission (Islam) as religion - never will it be accepted from him, and he, in the Hereafter, will be among the losers." (Q Aal-E-Imran 3:85)

The Quran eloquently summarizes the definition of religion as a way of existing, quoting its most popular verses with many interpretations. Furthermore, the pillars of subordination offer students a guide to follow and emulate. This enables them to practice mirror imaging and terminology while expressing the wonder they encounter and explore during their internal divine journey.

However, the primary anti-utopian organisms in the system are those who are given the choice to disrupt the harmony; the sons of Adam and Jinn. Corruption occurs when this educational tool is used for external consumption rather than divine mirroring of the universe itself. This leads to overconsumption, indulgence, greed, exclusivity, and the urge to subordinate others.

"The Lord said to the angels, 'Indeed, I will make upon the earth a successive authority.' They said, 'Will You place upon it one who causes corruption therein and sheds blood, while we declare Your praise and sanctify You?' Allah said, 'Indeed, I know that which you do not know.'" (Q Al-Baqarah 2:30).

"And He taught Adam the names—all of them. Then He showed them to the angels and said, 'Inform Me of the names of these if you are truthful.'" (Q Al-Baqarah 2:31).

The angels understood this aspect very well. However, Allah taught them that the purpose was the internal journey, and they would come to know.

The universe itself may fight back to restore the original default or send a message using its expression language, such as withholding rain or erupting volcanoes. The system is designed to submit to God first and then to Adam—unless Adam deviates. In such cases, the universe rebels, as it did with the people of all previous civilizations.

"Before them, the People of Noah rejected (their messenger): they rejected Our servant, and said, 'Here is one possessed!' and he was driven out. Then he called on his Lord: 'I am one overcome; do make me victorious.' So We opened the gates of heaven with water pouring forth. And We caused the earth to gush forth with springs, so the waters met (and rose) to the extent decreed. We bore him on an (Ark) made of broad planks and caulked with palm fiber. It floats under Our eyes (and care): a recompense to one who had been rejected." (Q Al-Qamar 54:9–14)

When a human walks, he sees a mirror of himself, and the horizon represents a mirror of himself.

"We will show them Our signs in the horizons and within themselves until it becomes clear to them that it is the truth." (Q Fussilat 41:53)

Imagine a group gathering around a fireplace on a moonlit night and reflecting. Although the horizon looks the same, everyone sees different images of themselves. Some may not care at all and delve into useless chatting, gossiping, or backbiting. Some fall asleep, and others are submerged in their sad past or scary future. A false spiritualist will see nothing but serenity that numbs and anesthetizes the natural journey to the truth. They might think that being calm is spiritual, enjoy a song, or do some breathing exercises and call it meditation. Others may gravitate lower and look for a partner to satisfy their ignited lust or desires. Some religious scholars may look for matching scripted verses of the horizon image and brag about their deep understanding and ability to recall and apply what they think they understand.

All these types of humankind see nothing but their 'selves'—whether non-ambivalent, self-absorbed, spiritually, or religiously deluded.

A few of them are truth-seekers. They escape from the falsehood of others' perceptions and explore the reality of the image created on the horizon, asking how it helps them understand the crafter of this image. Thus, the journey begins with interpreting the image by connecting with the Creator. However, the Creator has no comparison, and the universe is vast. The moon is beautiful, the stars are abundant, the fireplace provides warmth, and the stillness is serene. They realize that without the twinkling stars, the moon's silver light, and the fire's reddish hue, the scene would feel constraining and daunting. They come to the logical conclusion that beauty lies in light-configured images.

Eventually, they recognize that these guessing and reflecting procedures contribute nothing but mind-created beliefs, leaving them unsatisfied. But then they reflect on reflection itself and say, "We reached all these conclusions through a few logical internal reflections, and even though they are non-satisfactory, we realize that delving deeper than the mind might be the answer. But what other than a mind can think?" A verse in the Quran jumps immediately to the mind's internal horizon:

"Do they not have hearts that intellectually think?" (Q)

"So have they not walked through the earth and have HEARTS by which to reason and ears by which to hear? Indeed, it is not eyes that are blinded but blinded are the HEARTS within the chests." (Q Hajj 22:46)

Being overwhelmed by the intellectual hearts, they start calling the Creator Himself. They close their eyes to avoid being distracted by the majestic beauty and the delusional byproducts of the mind, and they invite the Creator to open their hearts' eyes and intellect. They seek the truth. To their surprise, the answer arrives from within. They see another vast horizon. This internal horizon hosts illuminated figures they can identify with, and they name them based on what they learned from the external horizon. They discover that this internal horizon is what the Quran repeatedly refers to as 'selves.'

They silently scream, "The universe is my educational mirror; the inside is myself." They feel an internal urge proclaiming that divine gnosis begins from within. The 'self' or internal horizon is nearer, more accessible, and the shortest path to the divine. They ponder about others, and the answer quickly follows: "Don't concern yourself with them. Mention My name so they can call Me, and I will teach you. Let others remain in their heedlessness, playful arena."

Others have already known themselves merely by gazing at the horizon. Yet, sadly, they don't recognize that the images blind them, and they continue down this path until they stray from the insightful internal journey.

"Say, 'Allah,' then leave them in their discourse, amusing themselves." (Q Anaam 6:91)

Chapter 11
"The Disclosure of Divinity in Divine Names"

In the preceding chapters, I examined the intricate concept of Lordship disclosure, proposing a nuanced distinction between Lordship and divinity. I suggested that while Lordship embodies a descended status characterized by a dynamic interplay of power and servanthood, divinity represents a state of absolute self-sufficiency and independence that fundamentally rejects notions of partnership or duality. In this context, Lordship acts as an essential intermediary, bridging the realms of conscious nothingness and the profound truths of the Divine. It carries the critical responsibility of delegating credentialing to others, known as *A'ghiar*, enabling these individuals to serve as instruments for acquiring wisdom about divinity and its many dimensions.

The phenomenon of Lordship can manifest itself in various ways, notably reflected in the horizon (*A'faq*) and within the intricacies of human existence (*Anfos*). This reflection is intended to convey a powerful parable of a unified, non-divisible, and self-sustained divinity that transcends our ordinary experience.

As I move into the forthcoming chapters, I will deeply explore the concept of divinity itself, unraveling its multifaceted nature and the broader implications it holds for our understanding of existence. I will employ a rich symbolic analogy to clarify this complex theme: The moon will represent the Lordship's revelation and characteristics, while the radiant sun will stand as a powerful metaphor for the essence of divinity. This vivid contrast not only serves to highlight the differences between the two concepts but also aims to illuminate the profound significance of divine presence and its crucial role in shaping our comprehension of higher realities. Through this exploration, I seek to better understand how Lordship and divinity interact within our spiritual journey and the insights they offer into the nature of existence.

To truly comprehend the profound origins of the love that gave rise to our existence, one must first grasp the essence of Allah's love, which flows eternally and unconditionally from Allah to Himself. This divine affection does not require humanity's acknowledgment or recognition. The Quran beautifully illustrates the unfolding journey of this love through a carefully arranged sequence of events intricately woven into the vast cosmic framework of heaven and earth.

In this divine narrative, Allah has fashioned two distinct realms of time for us to navigate through our sensory experiences: the life we currently inhabit and the life that awaits us after this earthly experience. These two realms are separated by a metaphorical night, a profound, deep sleep for our external senses, during which we transition back into the womb of Mother Earth, wrapped in her nurturing embrace. Here, the earth gently reclaims the dust of which we are made, reminding us of our humble origins while holding the sacred secret breathed into us—the essence of our being.

As we ponder this intricate cycle, we must consider that another version of our existence is already being crafted, preparing us to embark on a new journey, albeit under different laws and systems governing the life that follows.

To expand our understanding of this cosmic narrative, we might explore the concept of a non-spatial, non-temporal dimensional system that offers an alternative explanation. The idea of divine names and attributes serves as a cornerstone for understanding what this book refers to as the *"Veiling Dimension"*—a third dimension that is neither confined by space nor tethered to time constraints. It provides a deeper insight into the unfolding story of love and existence.

Names and Attributes: Allah's Parable is Incomparable Yet Illustrative

To explore the concepts of divine names and attributes, I will examine a few key names and their associated attributes as examples within the context of Allah's incomparable nature. However, He also possesses names that have likeness and comparability.

"There is nothing like unto Him, and He is all-hearing, all-seeing." (Q Al-Shura 11)

The key names are:

1. **The Ally (Al-Waly)**
2. **The Light (Al-Nour)**
3. **The Loving (Al-Moheb or Al-Wadood)**
4. **The Granter of Life (Al-Hayy)**

Allah's names are titles for His attributes, illustrating His deeds and actions. The *Spirit* (*Rouh*) represents a unique collective secret flowing within these attributes. While the spirit is singular, the attributes are numerous, each signifying a specific function that Allah reveals. Some attributes are more complex than others. The closer a name is to *Allah* in Quranic phrasing and writing, the more sovereign and collective it becomes.

The sequential methodology employed in studying Quranic word phrasing posits that the initial written name is more significant than the following names. This approach has led to the discovery of two names intricately connected to Allah's concept within various Quranic verses.

The first of these names is **"The Light" (Al-Nour)**. A notable example is the verse:

"Allah is the Light of the heavens and the earth." (*Q* Al-Nour 35)

This verse encapsulates the essence of divine illumination and guidance, emphasizing Allah's role as a source of clarity and truth, transcending the physical world.

The second name identified through this methodology is **"The Ally" (Al-Waly)**. This is illustrated in the verse:

"God is the ally to believers, taking them out of darkness into light." (*Q* Al-Baqara 257)

This passage highlights Allah's protective and supportive nature towards the believers, portraying a dynamic relationship where He guides them away from confusion and into spiritual enlightenment.

Together, these names deepen our understanding of Allah's attributes and His relationship with creation, illustrating His multifaceted role as a light source and a guardian to His followers.

The Ally (Al-Waly): The Guardian and Guide

In Arabic, divine names such as *"The Light" (An-Nur)* and *"The Ally" (Al-Waliyy)* hold profound significance, serving not only as titles of reverence but also as attributes that convey essential qualities of the Divine. The proximity of these names to Allah's name in the Quran's verses bestows upon them a layered collective meaning deeply rooted in Islamic theology.

When one examines the status of these titles, particularly concerning the designation of Adam and his descendants as *the deputy* (*Khalifah*), it becomes clear that the title of *Ally* offers a higher spiritual rank. For instance, in Surah Al-Baqarah (2:30), Allah states:

"Your Lord said to the angels: I am about to establish upon the earth a deputy."

This verse establishes human leadership and responsibility on earth, emphasizing the potential for Adam's descendants to take on this role as representatives of divine authority.

Delving deeper, the notion of *Allyhood (Wilaya)* brings forth a different dimension of this relationship. While all children of Adam may attain the role of a deputy through their actions and intentions, the embodiment of Allyhood is conferred upon a select few who achieve the most exalted form of deputyhood, known as *Awliyaa* (God's Allies).

Surah Yunus (10:62) states:

"Verily, God's friends (Allies) - they will have no fear, nor shall they grieve."

This verse highlights the unique relationship these individuals maintain with the Divine, offering them assurance and protection from fear and sorrow.

The identities of God's Allies among the descendants of Adam may range from the overt to the inconspicuous; they may be individuals who are widely respected for their piety or those who live in humility and obscurity, often dismissed by society. A well-known Hadith from

Sahih Muslim narrates: *"A person with shaggy and dusty hair, cast out from doors; if he swears by Allah, Allah makes it* happen.*"* This hadith illustrates that the criteria for being an Ally depend not on societal status, but on sincerity of faith and connection to God.

Furthermore, during the time of the Prophet Moses, the concept of deputy-hood was clearly embodied in his prophetic mission. However, a more profound, often hidden dimension of Allyhood exists, which Moses himself sought, represented by the enigmatic figure of Al-Khidr. The Quran narrates, *"And found one of Our servants, on whom We had bestowed grace from Ourselves and to whom We had imparted knowledge from Ourselves. Moses said, 'May I follow you on the condition that you teach me of that which you were taught for guidance"* (Qur'an, al-Kahf 65, 66). This encounter suggests that Moses, a great leader and prophet, pursued a spiritual understanding that transcended his evident role; he sought wisdom embodied by Al-Khidr, which signifies a hidden aspect of divine knowledge and guidance.

The function and essence of the Ally, as perceived through their attributes, can be likened to an extraordinarily subtle and secretive flow, much like the invisible currents within inert materials. Ally's qualities resonate with water's characteristics—colourless, tasteless, and essential for life—effectively nurturing all that exists and seamlessly adapting to various forms and tastes. This metaphor illustrates the profound yet often understated influence Allies can have, transforming their surroundings without seeking recognition. Imagine this in the context of a self-existing being, enveloped in an all-encompassing veil of brilliant white illumination, symbolizing purity, knowledge, and the concealed essence of the Divine guidance that flows through the Allies.

107

The Light (Al-Nour): The Source of Divine Illumination

Light is a powerful metaphor for a form of independent self-illumination reminiscent of the radiant and unwavering power of the sun. This celestial body shines brilliantly and consistently, independent of external influences or energy sources. This notion of self-sufficiency in illumination highlights the potential for inner truth and suggests an extraordinary clarity of vision that comes from within. Those who embody this light possess an inherent wisdom and understanding that enable them to navigate life's complexities with confidence and insight.

In contrast to this self-illuminated state, the role of *the Ally* is crucial. Allies function as beacons for others who seek enlightenment. By drawing from their light, Allies help guide and direct individuals toward greater understanding and wisdom. They provide support, insight, and encouragement, illuminating the path for those who wish to move out of their metaphorical darkness.

However, due to a misguided sense of entitlement and self-importance, some individuals resist the opportunity to seek illumination from the light represented by the Ally. These individuals may remain unaware that they dwell in darkness; instead, they might cling to a false sense of enlightenment. They often create an elaborate illusion that misleads both themselves and others, projecting an image of enlightenment while lacking the deeper understanding that true illumination brings.

As a result, these deceptive individuals can effectively manipulate their surroundings, crafting a façade that masks their lack of genuine insight. They may establish connections and relationships with those earnestly seeking truth and light, posing as partners on a shared journey toward enlightenment. In reality, however, they serve as false guides, disguised companions who distract from the path of proper understanding and personal growth. Their presence can lead genuine seekers astray, as the allure of their projected image may obscure the authentic light they genuinely yearn for. Thus, the journey toward enlightenment becomes complicated by such misleading figures, highlighting the importance of discernment in distinguishing authentic illumination from deceptive mimicry.

The Loving (Al-Moheb / Al-Wadood): The Essence of Divine Affection

Love encompasses two essential dimensions: self-love and love for others. These aspects are deeply intertwined within the spiritual framework of many beliefs, particularly in the context of Allah's nature as a loving being. The Quran beautifully articulates this theme:

"God will, in time, bring forth people whom He loves and who love Him." (Qur'an, Al-Maida 54)

Additionally, it emphasizes the importance of striving for excellence:

"God loves the doers of perfection (Mohseneen)." (Q Al-Baqara 195; Al-Imran 134; Al-Imran 148; Al-Maida 13)

This divine endorsement encourages believers to cultivate self-love and a deeper connection to their fellow human beings.

Furthermore, the *Hadith Qudsi*, especially cherished among Sufi communities, offers a captivating insight into the nature of divine love. It states:

"I was a hidden treasure, and I loved to be known, so I created a creation, and through Me, they recognized Me."

This profound declaration illustrates that love is not merely an emotion but an integral part of the divine essence that drives creation and fosters understanding.

In attempting to describe the manifestation of love, one can draw an analogy to fire, often seen as the closest representation of extreme and transformative love. For instance, the Messenger of God once asked Gabriel:

"Have you seen your Lord?"

Gabriel responded with a thought-provoking revelation:

"Between Him and me, Muhammad, there are seventy veils of light, and if I were to approach one of them, I would be burned." (Al-Masabih. Abu Nu'aim transmitted it in *Al-Hilya* on the authority of Anas)

This response illustrates the insurmountable nature of divine love, which is overwhelming to the extent that mere proximity to it would lead to annihilation.

The intense, consuming fire of love holds a paradoxical quality—it can obliterate the illusion of self and the existence of others in the first phase, known as the *"Annihilation phase"* on the spiritual journey. This stage is essential for spiritual awakening because it strips away the layers of the ego, revealing the true essence of love that exists beyond the individual self. However, such a profound transformation cannot occur without the benevolence of Allah's merciful attributes.

It is through this mercy that beings are granted life, as well as the consciousness necessary to recognize the illusion of separateness. This awareness is crucial in appreciating the arduous yet beautiful journey toward the ultimate realization of love.

Therefore, the spiritual path is a profound transition that guides individuals from the deceptive perceptions of an existence marked by nonexistence into a state of actual annihilation, where one realizes the reality of one's nonexistence within the fabric of existence itself. This journey from the illusionary realm to the ultimate truth is the essence of spiritual discovery, leading to a deeper understanding of love, both for oneself and for others.

The Life Granter:

The concept of death precedes the granting of life, elucidating a profound metaphysical relationship between the two states of existence. As articulated in the Quran, *"He brings forth the living out of the dead, and the dead out of the living"* (*Q* Al-Imran 27)

The aforementioned encapsulates a divine cycle in which death and life are interwoven into the fabric of creation. Another verse reinforces this idea:

"Allah is the One who cleaves the grain and the fruit-kernel asunder, bringing forth the living out of the dead, and He is the One who brings forth the dead out of what is alive. This, then, is God, and yet, how perverted are your minds?" (*Q* Al-Ana'am 95)

This passage illustrates the continuous interplay between existence and non-existence, urging the reader to reflect on the intricacies of divine wisdom.

Furthermore, the sacred question of existence is posed:

"How can you refuse to acknowledge God, seeing that you were lifeless, and He granted you life, that He will cause you to die and then bring you again to life, whereupon unto Him you will be brought back?" (*Q* Al-Baqara 28)

Here, the cycle of life is acknowledged, linking the transient nature of human existence to a greater divine purpose. The idea is reinforced in the verse, *"HE who was dead and We gave life, and We set up a light whereby he walks through people"* (Q Al-Ana'am 122), which alludes to a transformative experience, evoking the possibility of a renewed existence.

Delving deeper into the philosophical implications, death can be perceived as a distinct entity characterized by an innate intellect that allows it to understand its role within the continuum of life. When endowed with awareness, this 'nothingness' that is death may express an intense yearning to engage with the vibrant aspect of creation. This manifestation of intelligent death embodies a tumultuous desire, marked by imbalance, as it seeks to intertwine with the process of life.

However, such insatiable longing can give rise to arrogance and entitlement, causing death to momentarily overlook its dependency on the divine nature of creation. In stark contrast, the essence of divine love represents a pure and unfathomable force, devoid of any comparison. God's individuality, eternity, and unparalleled attributes establish an enduring truth that transcends earthly understanding. Within human comprehension, traces of divine love act as portals to deeper understanding, igniting passion and propelling creation forward.

The synthesis of these two intense forces —death's passionate yearning and divine love's nurturing essence —culminates in a transformative experience often referred to as the 'water of life.' This 'water' symbolizes the harmonious balance achieved through the merging of opposing forces and represents the initial catalyst that enables death to participate in reproduction, thereby producing new life.

Allah offers splendid illustrations of this process. Consider how flammable oxygen (O_2) and explosive hydrogen (H_2) combine to form water (H_2O), illustrating the delicate balance between volatile elements that enable the sustenance of life. Similarly, the cycle of rain nurturing barren earth to yield crops manifests divine love, awakening potential from lifelessness.

Within humanity, the sacred act of procreation stands as the quintessential representation of this cosmic dance of love and desire. By following divine commandments and the natural rhythms established by creation, the mating process inevitably leads to the emergence of new life—a pure and innocent child, reflecting the culmination of divine intent.

In conclusion, the 'water of life' represents the mysterious secret of creation and the vital element that enables death to participate in the continuous cycle of life. This interplay of divine love and death's yearning crafts a profound narrative, articulating the beauty of existence and the eternal dance between life and death.

Chapter 12
"Deviation in Divine Names Goodness and Perceived Evil"

Adam and the Totality of Divine Names:

In the initial creation phase, Adam was absorbed in the beauty of the totality of the divine names.

"And He taught Adam the names—all of them." (Q Baqara 2:31)

This totality is akin to the nectar or essence of the divine names, characterized by beauty and mercy. This mercy encompasses everything, including punishment.

"'I will smite with My punishment whom I will; yet My Mercy embraces all things. I will write it (My Mercy) to those who are cautious, give the obligatory charity, and believe in Our verses (Q Araf 156).

Note that the aforementioned verses provide a recipe for avoiding this self-inflicted punishment through the tools of piety, including giving charity and believing in divine verses.

This aspect of the divine names' totality is known as Goodness, and Allah's names revealed to express this goodness are referred to as 'Allah's names of goodness.' (*Asma Allah ul-Husna*)

"Whether you say a thing aloud or inaudibly, He knows the secret and the hidden. Allah! No God, there is but he. The names of Goodness are his." (Q Taha 20:7-8)

Adam was a reflection of this goodness and mercy; he embodied a mercy that bordered on naivety. He even heeded Satan's advice, never suspecting that anyone could tell lies. Allah warned Adam about excessive goodness and being absorbed in this phase of name totality by clearly cautioning him about Satan, which illustrated how poorly Adam's descendants would fare if they remained too naive to discern the tricks of the lower self.

Adam represented the totality of names and descended to Earth to understand that totality is the ultimate goal to uphold. As students learn in accounting schools, an expert in totality must also master itemization. Adam descended to Earth to explore the itemization of names. The learning process is modeled through the metaphor of descent, either by changing locations or, intriguingly, by shifting Adam's perception of himself, Satan, and the angels within his external horizon. However, Adam and the angels retained the ability to alternate their perception between the totality of names and the itemization of names, whereas Satan did not.

Satan became trapped in a phase of images until a specific time. Losing this ability is a curse upon Satan that will persist until the Day of Judgment.

"[Allah] said, 'O Iblees, what prevented you from prostrating to that which I created with My hands? Were you arrogant [then], or were you [already] among the haughty?' He said, 'I am better than him. You created me from fire and created him from clay.' [Allah] said, 'Then get out of Paradise, for indeed, you are expelled. And indeed, upon you is My curse until the Day of Recompense.' [Iblees] said, 'My Lord, then reprieve me until the Day they are resurrected.' [Allah] said, 'So indeed, you are of those reprieved, until the Day of the time well-known.'" (Q Sa'd 38:75-81).

If Allah is Good, Where Does Evil Originate?

What is the deviation in the divine names?

This question often perplexes people, potentially leading them to defy or deny the existence of God. Allah is good because He is One (*Ahad*), eternal (*Samad*), and unlike anything else. His mercy is overwhelming. When He created Adam as His deputy, He endowed him with the secret of His essence—totality. Evil begins to manifest when Adam's descendants pick and choose specific names to identify with instead of striving for the essence of those names.

"And (all) the Most Beautiful Names belong to Allah, so call on Him by them, and leave the company of those who deviate in His Names. They will be recompensed for what they used to do." (Q Araf 7:180)

This "deviation of the divine names" explains how evil arises; however, what is its purpose? This self-serving, biased, and imbalanced identification of one or more divine names over others represents a form of deviation and the source of all evil. It is a spiritual disease analogous to a self-inflicted chemical imbalance, such as the one resulting from indulging in alcohol, which may lead to atrocious outcomes.

This deviation is impossible for the collective name of "Allah" or the deputy-hood name of "The Merciful." These names are balanced and collective by default.

We all return to God or our initially created primordial self—the Muhammadian self. While our appearances as partial representations of divine names may differ across temporal or spatial contexts, we each complement one another to uphold the collective totality of that name. This signifies that we are both students and educational tools

116

for one another, assisting in the completion of our divine gnosis course.

"O mankind! We have created you from a male and a female and made you into nations and tribes that you get to know one another." (Q Hujorat 13)

Allah has made it easy for everyone to avoid the more complex, prolonged cycle in the afterlife. He has also provided a fair opportunity to change one's divine name representation. He has established a system for accomplishing this, as the complete representation of totality will eventually occur regardless. Furthermore, He has created a redemption system involving the sacrifice of money, the blood of animals, and efforts to redeem oneself, even by non-human entities that can be lifeless, such as stones.

"Then guard yourselves against the Fire prepared for disbelievers, whose fuel is men and stones." (Q Baqara 24)

The answer is that humankind should serve the divine name they have chosen by divine wisdom, but they must achieve balance within themselves. This balancing process is multifaceted. This task of balancing serves as an educational tool in itself, and it should be a foundational stage to initiate divine gnosis. Therefore, even those who seem evil can be a mercy to others by providing an opportunity to learn balance and a chance for themselves to begin the easier path toward goodness.

The itemized representation of the name is a quote (*Qawl*) that Allah ordained and will never change.

"The QUOTE will not be changed with Me, and never will I be unjust to the servants." (Q Qaf 29)

"Those upon whom the word will have come into effect will say, 'Our Lord, these are the ones we led to error. We led them to error just as we were in error. We declare our disassociation [from them] to You. They did not used to worship us.'" (Q Al-Qassas 63)

This previously mentioned verse in Surah Al-Qassas should be perceived as a happy ending to these people's misery, as their acknowledgment of self-error means they learned the lesson. Unfortunately, they will be initiated on the path of gnosis late, on a more extended day of the second life (*Hayat Akhera*), having wasted an opportunity on their first day; yet late is better than never.

The manifestation of this quote within the context of this chapter is the quote of itemized manifestations of the divine name's totality, which is declared and unchangeable. We are manifestations of the divine name's itemizations. We should aspire to reach the divine name's totality or at least be associated with those who have been granted this totality or balance the divine name with its opposite to achieve a balance that fosters mercy in this lower life. Otherwise, the need for balance will be imposed upon us in the afterlife, when our true selves will be more clearly displayed. We have the opportunity in this life to redeem ourselves by giving away things for the sake of goodness or by using deeds that Allah has ordained as "Good" (*Hasanat*) as a form of redemptive credit to attain balance in the afterlife. Since it is easier, more accessible, and less costly to do good deeds than bad ones, a person embodying evil in a divine name has a greater chance to balance their name with an opposing one to achieve a merciful state of equilibrium.

If an evil person knows which divine name counters theirs, Allah has declared a universal name for identification: *The Merciful. (Ar-Rahman)*

118

"Say, 'Call upon Allah or call upon the Most Merciful. Whichever [name] you call - to Him belong the best (goodness) names.'" (Q Al-Israa 110)

If another person has lost their willpower and fallen into despair, they can redeem themselves by uttering the statement of humble poverty to God: *"God, please forgive me." (Astaghfirullah).*

"Say, 'O My servants who have exceeded the limits against their souls! Do not lose hope in Allah's mercy, for Allah forgives all sins. He is indeed the All-Forgiving, Most Merciful.'" (Qur'an, Zumor 53)

"Inform My servants that it is I who am the Forgiving, the Merciful." (Q Hijr 49)

May Allah strengthen our connection with our master Muhammad and his family, just as He did with our master Ibrahim and his family. May Allah bless our master Muhammad and his family, just as He has blessed our master Ibrahim and his family.

Chapter 13
"The Divine Revelation of Love"

The Embodiment of Love:

The Love Journey Re-enacted

It is crucial to recognize that manifesting divine love does not equate to embodying God Himself. Throughout history, humanity has frequently created various personifications and familial structures for the divine, leading to conflicts over divergent interpretations and beliefs, sometimes culminating in tragic outcomes. This misinterpretation of divine embodiment has evolved alongside humanity and reached a significant point during the era of Jesus, the son of Mary, who ultimately became an object of worship. According to Islamic teachings, Jesus explicitly denies such deification, as noted in the Quran.

Surah Al-Maida, verse 116, states:

"God said: O Jesus, son of Mary! Did you say to people, 'Worship me and my mother as deities beside God?'" He replied, 'You are limitless in Your glory! It would not have been possible for me to say what I had no right to! If I had said this, You would surely have known it! You know everything within my 'self,' while I do not know what is in Your 'Self.' You alone fully understand everything beyond a created being's perception."

This exchange underscores the vital distinction between the divine and its earthly manifestations.

Grasping the intricacies of this creation process is fundamental for those pondering the underlying reasons for religious laws and regulations, including the ethical guidelines often described as 'dos and don'ts.' Moreover, this understanding provides a valuable framework for exploring the complex issues surrounding gender differences, particularly how these intersect with debates on equity versus equality.

Additionally, this exploration sheds light on humanity's deeply anchored desire for 'intelligent death'—a yearning to possess the very life that one generates. People tend to reject divine love as the ultimate source of existence unless reality exclusively belongs to it, i.e., intelligent death.

It also serves as an important counterpoint to those who might doubt the vivid representation of these existential truths in the afterlife. These truths are often interpreted as manifestations of human lust, sinful inclinations, and the active defiance or rejection of divine love. Religious texts symbolize this through illustrations of hellfire and the bitter consequences of sinful actions, contrasted with paradisiacal representations of legitimate existence, illustrated as the water of life's gracious by-product.

The narrative surrounding the journey of love provides a profound understanding of why individuals who are metaphorically 'dead' to divine truth often find themselves irresistibly drawn toward illicit desires and forms of self-worship. This tendency to prioritize personal gratification over divine love leads to significant spiritual imbalance.

Upon entering the afterlife, these individuals face a stark and often unsettling realization of their true existence. In this realm, they are compelled to confront the consequences of their choices with their entire being, leading to deep introspection about their past actions.

The internal struggles they experienced during their earthly lives begin to manifest outwardly. A significant decrease in modesty often symbolizes this process, as they claim to feel intense inner heat, which translates into less clothing and an increased inclination toward nudity.

The internal fires of lust and desire not only influence their behavior but also create a ripple effect, igniting the passions and desires of those around them. This lack of modesty and self-control fosters an environment where expressing these desires becomes more aggressive and prevalent.

Furthermore, the experience of the afterlife for these individuals may resemble a torturous existence within a hellish domain. They may find themselves surrounded by suffering and regret, echoing the painful truth of their choices. In this grim setting, they are confronted with a haunting statement from Satan himself: *"Don't blame me; blame yourselves."*

This statement resonates powerfully within the teachings of the Quran, serving as a reminder of personal accountability and the consequences of turning away from divine truth in life.

In this context, Satan serves as the archetype of conscious death, exerting a potent allure over those enslaved by this state. Although they may outwardly exist, these individuals frequently live in denial of their servanthood to the divine, often proclaiming their perceived freedom as they enter adolescence and grapple with various degrees of rebellion against God, whether by rejecting His sovereignty, disobeying His laws, or dismissing His messages. Ultimately, this denial leads them into a cycle of enslavement to their desires, tainting their perception with self-serving biases. This struggle results in a dangerous pull toward the satanic magnet, against which Allah warns humanity.

Surah Al-Israa, verse 62, states:

"He added: 'Tell me, is this whom You have exalted above me? Indeed, if You allow me respite until the Day of Resurrection, I shall certainly cause all but a few of his descendants to obey me."

During the formative phases of life, devoted seekers of the divine engage in tangible experiences to validate their spiritual journeys. They confront their desires, discipline their instincts, and navigate religious boundaries to ensure they do not overstep acceptable limits. These individuals often analyze their various experiences of love, ranging from longing to overwhelming passion, including the inherent void felt in the absence of original divine love. The pinnacle of this journey is often described as annihilation or 'Fana,' a state of merging with the Divine Presence.

The Quran encapsulates this transformative experience powerfully:

"All of what is over it will pass away. And there will remain only the face of Your Lord, Master of Majesty and Honour." (Q Ar-Rahman 27-28)

Furthermore, maintaining a connection with the Divine is emphasized:

"And keep yourself attached to those who call on their Lord, morning and evening, seeking His face." (Q Al-Kahf 29)

The reminder is clear:

"And do not drive away those who call upon their Lord morning and evening, seeking His countenance (face)." (Q Al-An'am 53)

These verses collectively invite individuals to seek a divine connection while acknowledging the transient nature of earthly existence.

It is essential to understand that progressing through the stations of love is a genuine, tangible, observable, and meaningful experience, not merely an overwhelming feeling or a sense of tranquility.

Chapter 14
"The Unveiling of Divinity"

The Concept of Veils (Partitions)

Veiling is to conceal beauty. Partitioning is for secretive dialogue.

The educational concept of veiling beauty suggests there is always something beautiful and precious to pursue. This pursuit requires time, effort, and resources. The veiled represents a valuable treasure. The effort that we put in pursuing the veiled rewards us with companionship and the joy of love.

The Lordship's educational methodology is evident in three key realms of our existence:

1. The physical realm (Mulk)
2. The illuminating spiritual realm (Malakoot)
3. And, the realm of invincibility (Jabaroot)

Lordship training and education are conducted through rules and regulations in the physical world of dos and don'ts (A'lam al-Mulk). These guidelines prepare individuals to move beyond the first veil of darkness, i.e., the self. Overcoming the veil of the dark lower self requires submission (Islam) of the external senses and recognition of the lower fire adorned with lust and desires. This concept is illustrated through gender regulations, where a woman must be veiled and is viewed as a prize. A man seeks her father's permission, pays a dowry, and presents gifts, leading to joy, companionship, and fleeting moments of ecstasy.

The Lordship educational method signifies the importance of a protective approach, especially for women during their formative years, by imposing a barrier of virginity. However, both men and women tend to deviate from the rules if the lower magnetic self of darkness prevails. In such cases, both men and women can get exposed to manipulation and misguiding caused by their dark lower selves. As a result, women may lose their virginity outside divine guidelines, diminishing the dowry's significance and being replaced by mere attention. This loss leads to the erosion of modesty's intangible veil, resulting in a tangible loss of virginity's physical barrier. Intimacy can degrade into fornication, and the understanding of the prize gets subjected to the delayed financial penalties. Innocent children may be caught in the crossfire, becoming instruments of revenge and destruction, reflecting how the dark lower self transforms into a false lord of darkness governed by Satanic reasoning. This evolution of the dark self came into existence with the creation of Satan and was revealed to Adam. Adam was directly cautioned about Satan's hostility toward him and his wife: *"Then We said, 'O Adam, this is an enemy to you and your wife; let him not drive you both out of the garden, lest you come to grief."* (Q Taha 118). *"But Satan caused them both to slip and drove them out from the state in which they were. Moreover, We said: 'Go forth; some of you are enemies of others, and for you, there is an abode on earth and provision for a time."* (Q al-Baqara 37) These steps involving the dark veils represent the pathway of Satan, distancing and veiling the truth: *"O you who believe! Submit wholly and follow not the footsteps of Satan; surely, he is your open enemy."* (Q al-Baqara 209)

The desires related to gender and the temptation of forbidden food were the first substantial lessons Adam and Eve learned the hard way. After eating from the tree, they followed Satan's footsteps and experienced an immediate humiliation of their exposure: "*So he caused them to fall into disobedience by deceit. Moreover, when they tasted the tree, their private parts became exposed to them, and they began to stitch together leaves in the garden to cover themselves. Their Lord called to them, saying, 'Did I not forbid you that tree and tell you that Satan is an open foe (enemy) to you?'*" (*Q* al-A'raf 23) Even mindlessly following Satan is described as Satanic worship: "*Did I not enjoin on you, O sons of Adam, that you worship not Satan? — for he is to you an open enemy.*" (*Q* Ya Sin 61)

Misguided reasoning, an unfounded sense of entitlement, an illusory notion of freedom, and harmful tendencies to share negativity, as well as profound ignorance, characterize the first veil that individuals must confront and overcome on their spiritual journey. Once they'd succeed in doing so, they would acquire proper illumination, develop divine companionship, and attain genuine understanding or gnosis.

This initial veil of darkness and ignorance marks humanity's default state. It reflects the profound challenge we face, as noted in the Quran: "*We offered the Trust to the heavens, the earth, and the mountains, but they refused to bear it and were afraid of it. However, humankind took on this burden, defaulting to darkness and ignorance*" (*Q* 33:73). This passage sheds lights on the weight of moral and spiritual responsibility accepted by the humanity despite its inclination toward ignorance.

How can we escape this inner darkness and the veils it creates? The answer is multifaceted; while this veil is an unavoidable aspect of our nature, it is also removable. However, its removal requires engaging in a rigorous struggle—a journey similar to navigating a battlefield, often referred to as self-struggle. In this situation, there is a lack of easy victories or win-win outcomes. The result must inevitably be a win-lose dynamic, where one aspect of the self must triumph over another.

The historical context provided by the battles during the time of the Prophet Muhammad (PBUH) is a powerful picturization of the challenges faced by oneself. These events reveal the significant veils we face in our internal battles. The opening of Makkah can be interpreted as a metaphor for the destruction of fake idols—both physical and ideological—and the revelation of profound truths symbolized by the Kaaba. I'd like to encourage readers to engage in a deep reflection on this analogy, as it offers rich insights into the spiritual path.

The veil of ignorance serves as a battlefield overwhelmed with well-armed soldiers of darkness, all under the leadership of Iblees, the personification of evil. The Hadith refers to this inner battle as Jihad al-Nafs or the struggle against one's desires and shortcomings. Following the opening of Makkah, the Prophet (PBUH) educated his companions in understanding the critical shift from the minor challenges of external conflict to the more significant and impactful struggle against the self.

For an individual on a spiritual path, it is essential to declare a metaphorical war on their inner self until it surrenders its defenses. These defenses often manifest as our external senses and their distractions. We can unlock the valid proof of reclaiming sovereignty over these vanquished senses by following a framework of ethical guidelines and principles known as Sharia law. This legal and moral structure provides crucial support in imposing a restraining order against the negative influences and misguided reasoning fostered by Satan.

The enforcement of this restraining order paves the way for an illuminating counterbalance to darkness, achieved through committed practices, such as regularly reading and reflecting on the Quran. The Quran encapsulates this dynamic by stating: *"And when you recite the Qur'an, We place a hidden veil between you and those who do not believe in the Hereafter"* (Q 17:46). This verse emphasizes the transformative power of divine words, creating a distinction between the enlightened and the ignorant. Thus, engaging with the Quran serves as a protective barrier and a source of enlightenment and clarity on the spiritual path.

This illuminated veil is similar to a radiant city that one creates. Spiritual seekers can verify it during their spiritual journey in the spiritual realm ('Alam al-**Malakoot**). The event's significant historical and physical manifestation occurred during the Prophet Muhammad's lifetime (PBUH/HF). This pivotal moment began with his migration from Makkah to Madina, a journey that symbolized a transition from a realm of darkness to utmost enlightenment. It marked a critical transition from verbal teachings to tangible actions and implementations of his message.

When the Prophet arrived in Madina, despite the heartwarming welcome of his devotees, he faced significant resistance, hostility, and disbelief from individuals driven by the forces of darkness and ignorance. His journey was not just a physical relocation; it was a separation from the oppressive environment of Makkah as he sought safety for himself and the early Muslims. He established Madina as the 'illuminated city' (al-Madina al-Munawwara) instead of simply referring to it as the 'good city' (Teebah). This designation emphasized the transformational light emanating from Madina, a place of refuge and enlightenment for the nascent Muslim community.

The Prophet (PBUH/HF) further enriched this narrative by declaring, "I am the City of Knowledge," as recorded in a hadith, emphasizing the importance of knowledge and enlightenment as central tenets of his message.

Moreover, Allah's intricate design of the universe serves as a powerful metaphor for this journey toward enlightenment. The lower illuminated sky that we witness is similar to a blackboard, where the principles of navigating through the veils of darkness, representing the ignorance of the self, are illustrated. This journey parallels the ascent from the depths of the ocean's darkness to the heavens' light. The Quran poignantly encapsulates this struggle:

"Or their deeds are like thick darkness in a vast and deep sea, which a wave covers, over which there is another wave, above which are clouds: layers of darkness, one upon another. When he extends his hand, he can hardly see it: and he whom Allah gives no light—for him, there is no light at all." (*Q* An-Nour 41).

This verse vividly depicts the confusion and despair that can be experienced when one lacks divine guidance. Allah encourages us to use the cosmic phenomena surrounding us as analogies, urging us to reflect on the signs within creation. This reflection can transform these hints into profound knowledge, providing invaluable guidance during our internal spiritual journey. However, this guidance is accessible only to "people who understand," as emphasized in the Quran:

"Verily, in the creation of the heavens and the earth and the alternation of night and day, in the ships that sail the sea with what benefits humanity, in the water that Allah sends down from the sky to revive the earth after its death, and scatters therein all kinds of creatures, in the change of winds, and in the clouds that serve between

heaven and earth—are indeed Signs for the people who understand."
(Q Al-Baqara 165).

The call to reflect on these elements invites individuals to deepen their awareness and appreciation of the divine signs ingrained throughout existence. Some people reject these signs or deliberately disregard them, despite clear evidence being provided by the Quran and history. This denial often stems from a preference for the veil of darkness that clouds external perception. The Quran addresses this tendency:

"And they say: 'Our hearts are under covers and are protected against that to which you call us, and in our ears, there is deafness, and between you and us, there is a veil. So carry on your work; we, too, are working." (Q As-Sajda 6).

This verse reflects the stubbornness of those who close themselves off from understanding and enlightenment. The spiritually illuminated journey through the internal cosmos, known as 'Alam al-Malakoot, unfolds truth in successive phases, revealing insights into various dimensions of enlightened existence. Throughout this journey, the seeker is guided by the metaphorical Star (Najm), navigating the intermittent phases of annihilation (Fana), the passing away of the self, within the layers of veils that obscure deeper truths, until finally arriving at the embrace of the 'Divine Face.' The Quran encapsulates this ultimate reality with the words:

"All that is on it will pass away (annihilate). And there will remain only the face of your Lord, Master of Majesty and Honour." (Q Ar-Rahman 27, 28).

This verse serves as a reminder of the transient nature of all worldly things and the enduring presence of the Divine.

Why is it essential to understand the veil analogy? Are there veil system simulations?

In the divine design of existence, Allah has established a model of veils that serve as guiding indicators for those seeking truth on their inner journey. These veils manifest as vivid yet obscure partitions of concealment, illustrating the complexities and nuances of the spiritual path.

Authentic hadith literature elaborates on this journey, indicating that the ultimate destination is symbolized by a blinding cloud, referred to as 'A'ma' or white-out. This overwhelming brightness represents a profound experience of divine presence beyond ordinary perception.

In an illuminating exchange, Abu Razin asked the Messenger of Allah a profound question: "Where was our Lord before He created creation?" The Messenger responded with striking imagery:

"He was enveloped in a blinding white-out ('ama'), with no air beneath Him and no air above Him. He established His Throne upon the waters in this state of singularity and transcendence."

This narration, found in hadith collections such as Tirmidhi, emphasizes the majesty of Allah's existence before creation and serves as a reminder of the mysteries surrounding the divine and the journey of faith.

He meticulously constructed a series of intricate simulations: a vast, multidimensional universe designed to mirror the cosmos we inhabit, a profound historical journey through the significant eras and events of various nations, and a multitude of reenactments intended to impart wisdom about enduring tales of love and sacrifice.

Imagine, if you will, a self-igniting treasure concealed beneath layers of obscurity, shrouded by a relentless blizzard of pristine white. The outermost veil surrounding this treasure is an all-consuming, annihilating fire that embodies passionate love, while a gentle breath of mercy tempers this ferocious blaze. This delicate balance produces swirling black smoke laced with sediments of dust, mud, and clay, representing the complexities of existence. These veils do not merely represent the creation of humanity; they reflect the very structure of the cosmos itself.

In the Quran, this creation is encapsulated beautifully in the verse that describes the genesis of the skies from smoke:

"He applied His design to the skies, which were smoke; and He said to them and the earth, 'Come, both of you, willingly or unwillingly!' To which both responded, 'We do come in obedience." (Q Fussilat 11).

The phases of Adam's creation relate to this concept, signifying that the earth's fundamental components—dust, mud, and clay—played a crucial role, similar to the creation of malevolent spirits that stemmed from the dense black smoke of fire. The scripture states:

"He has created man out of sounding clay, like pottery; whereas the invisible evil beings have been fashioned out of a black exhaust of fire." (Q Ar-Rahman 14, 15)

Furthermore, it emphasizes:

"Your Lord said to the angels: I am about to create mortal man out of sounding clay, out of dark slime transmuted" (Qur'an, Al-Hijr 28). This heavenly narrative continues, showcasing the raw material of humanity when it declares, *"As for the nature of Adam, whom He created out of DUST and then said to him, 'Be' - and he is"* (Q Al-Imran 59).

133

The grand cosmic construct is composed of seven majestic heavens, where the ethereal light of mercy penetrates the enveloping smoky darkness that blankets the atmosphere, igniting the spark of life through the rain. The foundational layers of earth, crafted from dust, mud, and clay, emerge as seven distinct piles, each layer a sign of the diminishing presence of mercy. This transformation is characterized by a gradual decrease in freshwater, an increase in acidic liquids, and a rise in heat intensity, culminating in properties reminiscent of the original, formidable fire veil, which exemplifies the slightest manifestation of mercy found in the seventh layer of the earth.

The interaction between water and fire generates a mixture of black smoke and dust particles. Dust and water merge to form mud. Here, the uncontrollable heat from the eternal fire of love manipulates the mud into malleable clay, shaping the raw essence of creation and the narrative of existence itself.

Chapter 15
"Spiritual Navigation to the Divine Love"

Creation of Humankind (Nas) and the Evil-Spirited Kind of Jinn

Allah granted conscious existence to many creatures so they could experience a journey of love while searching for it. He informed us about two fundamental creations:

1. Humankind (Nas), made from mud and clay
2. Fire spirits (Jinn), created from the black smoke of fire

Consequently, both Jinn and Nas originate from the interactions of love, fire, and water; however, Nas is drawn toward the fire of love, approaching the illuminated whiteness. Simultaneously, Jinn is attracted downward toward an enduring flame.

In life after death, the depiction of this model as heaven becomes clearer, signifying proximity to the divine secret. Hell signifies separation from the divine, symbolized by a distant fire. Contrastingly, the straight path connects the reunited beings across the flames of Jahannam.

When the Jinn and Nas have choices during their first life on Earth, the distant fire manifests as lust, desires, and sinful behavior. The upper fire of love and warmth manifests through phases of annihilation into truth or false non-existence (Fana and Baqa'). The journey from the fire of desires to the fire of love is a magnificent spiritual wayfaring experience referred to as spiritual navigation (Sulook). The guidance of prophets, messengers, and God's allies

(Awliyaa) is essential for the truth seeker to remain on the straight path (Sirat Mustaqeem).

Navigating the Straight Path:

In the first chapter of the Quran (Al-Fatiha), we pray to Allah to guide us to the straight path (Sirat Mustaqeem), moving from the distant fire to the closeness of love in every unit of prayer. Reciting Al-Fatiha is essential for validating our prayers.

According to authentic Hadith, during the reckoning phase in the afterlife, the straight path appears as a narrow pathway—sharper than a sword and thinner than a hair—that stretches above a blazing fire.

Both humans (Nas) and Jinn reside where they concluded their first lives. Although they appear to reside in the same state, their differing manifestations reveal the deeper meanings of Gnostic teachings more clearly.

In Sharia rituals, immersing in or showering with water is a necessary cleansing process after intimate sexual interactions. This act symbolizes how the water of mercy should extinguish the fire of desire before we resume prayer, eating, and other daily activities.

Their dimensional thinking often limits humankind's understanding. Throughout their spiritual journey, seekers realize that divine knowledge transcends the human mind's capacity.

For example, Allah is all-encompassing, which means He transcends all limitations, and nothing is beyond His ability to comprehend:

"All the while, God encompasses them without their awareness." (Q Al-Bourooj 20)

Allah is the Most High (Al-A'laa), and nothing exists below Him; depth does not apply to His nature:

"And He alone is truly exalted (Most High), the Great." (Q Al-Baqara 255)

Therefore, Allah has instilled in humanity a framework of dimensional thinking. This framework requires the emergence of existence from nothingness, a process that relies on intellect to transform an idea into a tangible reality. Thus, all things begin as nothingness endowed with intellectual potential.

The mind must understand that the directional concepts of up and down, left and right, are created for spiritual navigation in a vertical sense, while the cardinal directions of North, South, East, and West serve for horizontal navigation in the material world.

Allah mentioned His Spirit in Adam's creation story:

"When I have formed him fully and breathed into him of My spirit, fall before him in prostration!" (Q Sad 72)

This moment illustrates the profound connection between the Creator and His creation, signifying the divine essence that infuses life into humanity.

Furthermore, Allah's reference to His 'Self' is striking:

"But God warns you to beware of His 'Self,' for with God is the end of all journeys." (Q Al-Imran 28)

This verse serves as a reminder of the ultimate reality that lies beyond human comprehension, urging us to acknowledge the profound nature of the Divine.

In Islamic belief, Allah is the Truth, with nothing existing alongside Him. However, this notion of nothingness is not one of independent existence; instead, it serves as a canvas upon which Allah's attributes are reflected, like shadows cast by an illuminating light.

When a community recognizes the distinctions that set its members apart, revealing this abstract knowledge demands articulation through descriptions, quotes, and comparative references. Without such expressions, these unique qualities remain veiled and inaccessible. Each individual possesses a unique essence—a singularity—which distinguishes them from others.

A bridge is required to transform this unimaginable singularity into comprehensible descriptions. The human intellect represents this bridge—the translator that disassembles knowledge into myriad expressions while tracing back to a single reality. Each group member may internalize their singular quality, portraying it through various forms, such as a painting, a novel, a culinary recipe, a poem, a strategic plan, or any other creative expression.

For external expressions to manifest, imagination and intention must first ignite a desire, accompanied by a spoken word that catalyzes the subtle flow of this creative energy. The translator, or intellect, must discern, articulate, and bring these manifestations into the world.

Within this framework:

- The 'Singularity' is the 'Secret of the Secret'
- The flow of creativity is the 'Secret' or 'Divine Spirit'
- The intellect serves as the 'Divine Self'
- Divine attributes represent the descriptions
- Unique expressions of divine attributes are the Divine Names

The command 'Be' functions as the crucial message or release word, facilitating the journey from a singularity (Ahadiya) to the 'Secret' or the Spirit (Rouh). This Spirit carries the 'Message' to the translating intellect (Nafs), which then performs the act of manifestation in diverse shapes, colors, and names. This process moves from a singularity to a multitude of expressions.

To clarify this concept further, we can use the sun as a powerful metaphor for the manifestation process. The sun's core symbolizes the enigmatic and ineffable essence—the singularity that contains profound secrets beyond the realm of sensory perception. This singularity embodies an ultimate truth akin to an unfathomable source of energy and creation that remains hidden from direct experience.

Surrounding this luminous center is an intense light that radiates outward, forming an intermediate layer—a bridge connecting the core truth with our more tangible reality. This layer signifies the nature of the secret, embodying the spirit or an allied reality that serves as a portal for the central truth to reach the outer world.

As we move further away from the sun's center, we encounter its rays, representing the dispersion of the profound message into various unique manifestations. These rays symbolize the diverse interpretations and expressions of the divine essence, each capturing distinct aspects of the singularity from which they originate.

To illustrate this dynamic interplay more vividly, consider a specific divine name comparable to an ultraviolet ray, marked by its distinct and elusive properties that can only be detected through specialized instruments. At the same time, we might envision a divine attribute presenting itself in a more tangible form, such as the gleam of bronze skin, which radiates vibrancy and richness—an effect created by light interacting with matter. This complex relationship highlights how the essence of the core truth manifests in various perceivable forms, deepening our understanding of the intricate fabric of existence and reality.

Similarly, the message of love is continuously sent from the singularity and diverges into various attributes and names. The sun's heat radiates from the sun to the sun. We serve merely as intellectual beneficiaries of this self-igniting, magnificent lamp, which remains indifferent to appreciation or disappointment. Likewise, the message of love comes from Allah to Allah. We are simply beneficiaries who neither add nor subtract anything from the overall process. The external manifestation of the message of love reveals the fundamental role that 'nothingness' plays as a blank slate, reflecting the message of love through a broader range of names, images, and analogies. This manifestation follows another process within the boundaries of 'nothingness.'

Due to its very nature, nothingness cannot be considered divine. However, we are provided with a limited form of pseudo-intellect through the gift of conscious awareness and perception. This awareness enables us to explore and engage with the depths of existence, even in the presence of the void. As we perceive and interpret the world around us, we assign meaning to our experiences, challenging the notion of nothingness and opening pathways for understanding and enlightenment.

Seeing without savour ignites a deep yearning for more—a sense of pride, a desire to possess this message of love exclusively, and a need to break free from the constraints of regulated love. It culminates in a state of arrogance, lust, and uncontrollable passion, where we disregard boundaries and defy rules, all while maintaining this sense of 'nothingness' in 'Darkness' that yearns for Allah's divine love. Moreover, since Allah is 'Light,' the ultimate revelation of this love message must illuminate, causing these dark manifestations to recede and leading the consciousness to feel hurt and disappointed.

The gift of 'nothingness' creates a sense of entitlement, leading to a false belief that it is the deputy receiver of divine light. Since Allah is 'Light,' this results in the incorrect assumption that it must represent the reality of Allyhood, as Allah is the 'Ally.' However, nothingness and darkness that diminish in the presence of the love's illuminating message ultimately quash these desires, leaving behind resentment toward the light receiver or deputy.

Then, a beautiful message of love emerged from the secret of singularity, like a radiant sun lighting up the intellectual horizon of darkness. This message was embraced by the Secret, or the Spirit (Rouh), which joyfully affirmed that the representative of Allyhood (Wilaya)—who translates divine light—is a harmonious blend of both light and darkness. They are formed from the tempered fire of passion and the gentle water of mercy, carefully crafted from clay dust.

This intellectual, proud, arrogant, lustful, boundary-seeking and exclusive dark nothingness acquired a hope that the command would change—a gift rooted in the clay component. This quality is called envy. The intellectual nothingness expressed animosity toward the illuminated, magnificent clay creation. Furthermore, it recognized that it was a part of the clay's formation, making it an attractive magnet for the dark side of the illuminated clay. However, it did so by sharing intellect and sending messages of non-love to its enemy and clay-made rival.

This story is not a Greek myth. It is recounted, reenacted, and personalized multiple times in the Quran. Adam is created from clay, infused with light, and capable of forming a friendship with God. He is prone to darkness yet aspires to light; he is obedient but sinful, a wrongdoer who repents, and a balanced keeper of divine names and attributes. He is able to guide others to light and away from darkness.

In contrast, there exists the intellectual, envious, proud, and eternal enemy of humankind—a mind-sharer and thought-whisperer, a friend of darkness (Taghoot) who leads others from light into darkness. This figure is known as Satan.

"Those who are bent on denying the truth are the powers of evil (Taghoot) that take them out of the light into deep darkness: it is they who are destined for the fire, therein to abide." (Qur'an, Baqara 257)

"Who whispers in people's hearts." (Q Nas 5)

Chapter 16
"Divinity and Sun Analogy"

I am captivated by the parable of the Eternal Sun, a metaphor that embodies both the concealed and revealed aspects of divinity. This Sun, shrouded in exquisite veils of beauty, profound love, and tempered fire, radiates warmth and illumination while remaining elusive. Despite its all-encompassing nature, it is also immersed in the waters of Mercy, symbolizing boundless compassion that nurtures all existence.

Divinity is a vast and complex topic that is often overlooked in discussions due to its inherently metaphorical and metaphysical qualities, which transcend the limits of human comprehension. This complexity leads to the concept of non-comparability, known as Tanzeeh. Tanzeeh asserts that the essence of the Divine cannot be fully articulated in our limited language and understanding. To bridge this gap, we must resort to analogous parables—referred to as Tashbeeh—that employ the method of 'as if' to draw parallels that hint at a deeper truth.

Picture a series of concentric circles made of ethereal veils, each layer representing an aspect of existence that both conceals and reveals the Divine. At the center of these circles lies the absolute truth, shimmering softly yet profoundly within its mysterious core.

At the heart of existence lies a central truth—an enigmatic reality known only to itself. This truth possesses an innate love and admiration for its exquisite beauty—a profound love that catalyzes movement within the vast expanses of nothingness. This movement transforms nothingness into intricate circles, each layer serving as a veil that manifests the various aspects of existence.

The first of these circles is the veil of whiteout, known as A'ma'. This circle represents the initial expression of love—an ethereal and luminous embodiment that envelops everything in a breathtaking, cloudy expanse of white. It embodies pure goodness and is often referred to as "the Chair," a throne for the divine essence. In this serene and radiant space, the beauty of creation shines brightly, drawing forth the adoration of all it touches.

Surrounding this veil of whiteout is the fierce and transformative fire of love, which engulfs it in an explosive, vibrant energy. This fire is not destructive; rather, it is an invigorating force that adds layers of intensity and passion to the already-existing beauty. The flame dances and flickers with an uncontainable fervor, creating a complex interplay of light and shadow that enhances the allure of the white veil.

Beyond this fiery embrace lies the circle of black smoke, a stark contrast to the brilliance of the love veil. This darkened sphere symbolizes the remnants of burned-out nothingness, a shadowed realm formed as the fiery essence recedes. The interplay of despair and absence becomes palpable within this blackened veil, representing a profound depth of existence marked by forsakenness and silence.

The next layer, the veil of density, further encapsulates the experience of nothingness. This circle embodies absolute emptiness, yet it is not devoid of significance. Instead, it is tempered by the surrounding mercy that envelops it—a gentle yet powerful force that exists even in despair. This mercy serves as a protective buffer, hinting at the concealed truths that await uncovering amidst the void.

Finally, we arrive at the veil of total encompassment with Mercy. This circle represents a nurturing embrace akin to the soothing sensation of cool, refreshing water. It signifies a profound mercy that washes over all layers of existence, offering solace and calm. This grace can be likened to being **"thrown"** into a vast ocean of compassion, providing assurance and comfort even in the midst of chaos.

Together, these circles of veils illustrate the layered complexities of existence, where love, light, darkness, and mercy intertwine. They reveal the detailed beauty of the truth at the heart of all creation.

When we contemplate the vastness of the cosmic structure surrounding us, we realize that Allah has intentionally designed all of creation so that we may perceive and understand Him. He has provided us with subtle hints and illuminating parables that beckon reflection. However, this awareness is reserved for those who genuinely ponder the grandeur and intricacy of the heavens and the earth, recognizing that this immense universe is not just a playground for amusement or a fleeting spectacle.

The dense and tactile earth, coupled with the expansive darkness of the sky, reveals a more profound significance, especially when we consider the radiant celestial bodies that serve as luminous guides. These illuminating lamps, alongside the ethereal beauty of white clouds contrasting **against** the profound darkness **of** the ocean's depths, convey a profound message about existence and divinity.

With its scorching heat, the sun symbolizes an approach to the divine. It offers warmth and illumination, yet this warmth is only experienced when we maintain a certain distance, illustrating the balance required in our spiritual approach.

Adam's creation, originating from the densest point of this earthly realm, highlights a critical paradox: within his being lies both the secret of the divine and the potential for animosity, originating from the higher realms represented by the black smoke of the Satanic archetype.

This intricate relationship may shed light on Iblees's arrogance. Through misguided reasoning, Iblees viewed himself as superior to Adam, the denser form. However, he failed to comprehend that Adam, by his creation, is intrinsically closer to the circle of divine mercy, which exists beyond the central reality. This proximity affords Adam the most direct pathway to the divine essence.

Yet, Adam's journey is not without its challenges. He must navigate through various veils that obscure his path to the divine. It begins with an intense struggle against the self, similar to the pull of a satanic magnet that seeks to divert him from his true purpose. From this initial struggle, Adam's ascent continues through various spiritual stations, culminating in the transformative fire of love. This force purifies and elevates him closer to understanding and unity with the divine.

This entire process illustrates the intricate dance between the material and the spiritual, guiding Adam—and, by extension, humanity—on their quest for divine connection and comprehension.

May Allah strengthen our connection with our master Muhammad and his family, just as He did with our master Ibrahim and his family. May Allah bless our master Muhammad and his family, just as He has blessed our master Ibrahim and his family.

Chapter 17
"The Soul, The Self, and The Heart"

Return Journey from Earthly to Ethereal

In Islamic theology, Allah's likeness is an insightful and extremely layered concept of singularity and incomparability. Despite His Oneness, Allah has revealed aspects of His essence, including His names and attributes, to facilitate a deeper understanding of His majestic and enigmatic nature. This revelation is significant because Allah's names possess transcendental qualities that go beyond the limits of human comprehension and imagination.

In the grand scheme of creation, humankind possesses two unique advantages over other beings: the ability for outward expression and understanding, as highlighted in the verse, "*He created humankind. He taught him clear expression*" (*Q* ar-Rahman 4-5).

Additionally, humans have been entrusted with the Divine Spirit, as stated, "*Your Lord said to the angels, I am creating a skin-covered creature from dry, ringing clay, from black mud. When I have perfectly fashioned him and breathed into him of My Spirit, prostrate in submission to him*" (*Q* al-Hijr 30).

Through the names and attributes designated by Allah, humans can explore concepts, share knowledge, and gain insights. The richness of language and expression empowers individuals to articulate thoughts and teachings that draw others closer to the essence of Allah. The Ninety-Nine Names, or the Names of the Best Goodness, reflect Allah's likeness; each name represents distinct attributes vital for a foundational understanding of gnosis or spiritual knowledge. These names serve as essential tools for contemplation and learning, encompassing divine characteristics such as mercy, forgiveness, wisdom, and power, all of which reflect Allah's multifaceted glory.

The Quran often emphasizes divine names at the end of verses to highlight significant teachings: *"And if Allah wills, He could have put you to hardship. Allah is Mighty and Wise."* (Q al-Baqara 221), and *"Allah is the Most Forgiving, Merciful."* (Q al-Baqara 174).

Do the Divine Spirit and Self Represent Divine Essence or Names and Attributes?

In one of Sheikh Muhammad Faouzi Al-Karkari's poems, he expertly illustrates the divine names as flowers and depicts the Spirit as nectar. In this analogy, if we consider the divine names as flowers, the Self would distribute and reveal their sacred, unique nectar. In this context, the nectar symbolizes the "Spirit."

Allah refers to His Spirit and His Self. He consistently imbues the Spirit with descending knowledge and revelation:

"The Trustworthy Spirit has descended with it" (Q as-Shura 194). *"On the day when the Spirit and the angels will stand in rows, they shall not speak unless permitted by the Merciful"* (Q an-Naba 39).

Furthermore, the Spirit is designated with the male pronoun, contrasting with the female pronoun of the Self, which is associated with cautionary warnings:

"Allah cautions you against His Self; and towards Allah is the destination" (Q Al-Imran 29).

"Allah warns you about His Self. And Allah is Most Gentle with His servants" (Q Al-Imran 31).

Just as He categorizes divine gnosis into names and attributes, Allah presents His Spirit and Self as an intriguing collection of books comprising two mirror-image volumes, each containing seven chapters. Both volumes convey the same story, albeit in different ways. Furthermore, He revealed this book on the cosmic horizon and within humankind's 'selves.'

The Quran beautifully and clearly illustrates this 'book': *"We shall roll up the heavens like the rolling up of written scrolls of a book. As We began the first creation, so shall We repeat it. A promise binding upon Us; We shall certainly perform it." (Q al-Anbiya 105).*

The Quran invites us to observe the open book on the horizon and the personal book within ourselves to attain pure, fresh, and untainted knowledge of Allah's essence. Furthermore, Allah refers in the Quran to realms beyond perception, such as the existence of seven inhabited layers of heaven and, correspondingly, seven inhabited layers of Earth, the extraordinary that may resonate: *"We will show them Our Signs in the horizons and within themselves until it is clear to them that He is the truth." (Q as-Sajda 54).*

Bringing together manifestations of Spirit and Self from the horizon to the human self and beyond illustrates the interplay of various elements in both the heavens and the earth: the lowest illuminated heaven and barren earth; pairs of opposites such as men and women, males and females; the human soul and the human self; the anatomical upper and lower body; love and desire, and so forth.

The Karakriya Sufi Order and the System of Secrets

In the 21st century, within the Karakriya Sufi order, Sheikh Mohammad Fouzi Al-Karkari (may Allah sanctify his secret) has meticulously formulated a comprehensive system for acquiring knowledge to guide seekers in exploring their inner selves. This intricate framework, the System of Secrets, is founded on the concept that true enlightenment arises from a profound, introspective journey. As seekers delve into their internal landscapes, they awaken to a heightened level of consciousness, signifying a significant exploration of their true essence. Upon achieving this awakened state, they are bestowed with a status within a hierarchy of seven secret levels, ranging from first to seventh, each representing a deeper understanding of spiritual truths.

Furthermore, Sheikh Al-Karkari recognizes that some seekers may not yet attain full enlightenment but can achieve a partial status known as a 'reading' into the secrets. These readings act as glimpses into mystical knowledge and vary in number, often representing seven or multiples of seven. This results in a diverse community of secret holders among Karakriya disciples, each identifying themselves along a spectrum, ranging from those deeply rooted in self-awareness to those who resonate more fully with the spirit's ethereal dimensions.

As truth seekers navigate this transformative journey, they gradually come to realize a profound truth: the universe is not just an external entity, but an integral part that mirrors their own being. The internal pursuit of divine secrets emerges as one of the most accessible and direct pathways to enlightenment available to humanity. The essential teaching emphasizes that individuals need only cultivate a willingness to engage with the wisdom in this sacred text and aspire to transcend the limitations imposed by their self-image. This process encourages them to elevate their consciousness from the dense realms of the self to the enlightened planes of their spirit, effectively bridging earthly existence with the heavenly experience within their lifetimes.

If one neglects this opportunity in the present life, they may face a poignant reality on the **Day of Judgment** in the afterlife. After a brief rest in the grave, they will inevitably return to this profound book of wisdom. Upon their return, the secrets will unfold with a more apparent and majestic revelation, thus presenting a narrative of enlightenment that may not always be comfortable or pleasant. Hence, the urgency of the journey becomes apparent, prompting seekers to fully embrace their exploration of the secrets within before the cycle recommences anew. *"Read your book. Your SELF this day is a sufficient reckoner against you."* (*Q* Israa 15). *"The Book of the Wicked is in a place of incarceration. What should you know about the place of incarceration? It is a digital book. Woe to those who reject that day!"* (Q Mutaffifeen 8-11). *"The Book of the Righteous is in a high place. What should you know about the high place? It is a digital book, witnessed by those close by."* (*Q* Mutaffifeen 19-22).

Embarking on the Journey from Earthly Self to Ethereal Spirit Realms

Allah repeatedly indicates in the Quran that we will indeed return to Him, and the destination is with Him. *"To Allah is the final destination" (Q Al-Imran 3),* *"and to you is the destination"* (*Q* al-Baqara 286). *"Those who know they will meet their Lord and that to Him will they return"* (*Q* al-Baqara 47), and *"But they have become divided among themselves in their affair, and all will return to Us"* (*Q* al-Anbiya 94). Allah praises those who remember their divine destination while facing calamities, saying, **"When a mishap overtakes them, they say: We belong to Allah, and to Him shall we return"** (*Q* al-Baqara 157).

Devoted Sufi truth seekers engage deeply with the Quran, interpreting its teachings in the context of their present experiences. For them, the

Quran is not merely a historical text but a dynamic and contemporary guide for their internal quest. They believe it's wisdom can be applied to current circumstances while connecting the dots to their transcendent experiences.

This approach involves profound reflection on how the Quran's verses resonate with personal journeys. It offers insights that help navigate the complexities of sensible illusion while remaining rooted in a specific spiritual journey. Relating the Quran's timeless messages to their meditational experiences gives seekers a sense of purpose and direction.

Therefore, the starting point for grasping the concept of the divine dual collective—names and attributes of the Spirit and the Self—through the analogous physical realm and human manifestations within the context of the Quranic metaphorical narrative leads to the conclusion that we are essentially swimming, diving, and ascending in a vast ocean of spirit manifestations known as the sky while resting on a dense representation of the divine Self, only separated by an illuminated atmospheric barrier that obscures the path in between. Prostration perfectly depicts this starting point by placing the forehead on the earth, dust, or stones.

Interestingly, one of the most rewarded two-word phrases in Arabic is **"Subhan Allah"**, which translates to **"What a Divine swimming!"** However, people often interpret it as exaltation or praise to Allah due to a lack of deeper understanding. Saying **"Subhan Allah"** is akin to sowing in paradise and carries significant weight on the scale of deeds in the afterlife.

Therefore, we essentially serve as the link between the vivid imagery of our external senses, which represent manifestations of the Self, and the inward expression of our Spirit, communicated through our internal senses. This journey takes us from the earthly realm to the ethereal one, and we should approach it with open hearts.

The Journey to Truth is Internal

Exploring the Divine Self begins with examining oneself—or one's many selves—followed by searching within to find one's purest form. Subsequently, the seeker rises to explore their Spirit, which is simply the Divine breath from the Creator's Spirit that granted Adam a master status over the angels. Once the seeker excludes the additional imperfect selves they have produced, identifies with the pure, singular, original Self, and recognizes and witnesses their Spirit, they can attain Divine gnosis.

As mentioned, the starting point originates from the external physical realm, as Allah established Earth as a transient respite. The seeker's submission (Islam) of their Self to the Divine Self begins with the physical act of prostration, where the forehead touches the Earth element representing the Divine Self, EARTH. In Sharia law, any dry earth element is pure and can be used as a water alternative for dry ablution (**Tayammum**) before commencing the act of prayer. It means that the earth's dry element is as pure as clean water, representing the Divine self's manifestation.

The Quran describes the physical act of prostration on Earth as a means to draw near to God: *"Prostrate yourself and draw near"* (*Q* Al-Alaq 20). Ritualistically, prostration represents the closest anyone can get to the Divine Self, serving as a gateway to embark on an internal journey. Furthermore, prostration was a direct command given to Mary, instructing her to prostrate before kneeling. The Quran states, *"O Mary, be obedient to your Lord, prostrate, and kneel with those who kneel"* (*Q* Al-Imran 44). This ritual of physical submission to the external senses is mandatory five times daily for the Adamic Self to open the path to the Divine Self.

Submission and the Path to the Spirit

In addition to the five daily declarations of submission through prostration, the outward training of the personal Self in the physical realm takes place once a year, focusing on two lower desires: gluttony and lust. This training involves abstaining from food, water, and sexual relations during daylight hours. Such practice suggests an internal journey that becomes clearer when the "**Sun of Truth**" rises, illuminating the heart of the spiritual wayfarer. In Sharia, missing one day of fasting during the month of Ramadan carries significant consequences; it is penalized by requiring the individual to fast for two additional months, free a slave, or feed 60 people. It emphasizes the seriousness of neglecting the sovereignty of the Divine Self when it is close and accessible. By momentarily resisting lower desires and gluttony, one honors this connection.

The daily and annual practice of outward submission of the Self serves as a vital foundation for the truth seeker, preparing them for the next crucial phase: the submission of the heart (**Qalb**). This deep inner submission acts as a bridge, facilitating the journey from confronting and purifying the Self (Nafs) to ultimately forging a connection with the Spirit (ar-Rouh).

Within the heart lies a unique switch that connects the Self with the Spirit. This switch can be compared to a key, prompting one to seek permission to enter a complex maze and guiding one closer to the heart's core. A significant manifestation of this spiritual journey is the pilgrimage known as the Hajj, which every able Muslim is obliged to undertake at least once in their lifetime.

Hajj: A Migration of the Heart

Hajj represents more than a physical journey; it is a profound declaration of the heart's submission to the Divine Self. This sacred pilgrimage demands considerable effort, unwavering dedication, and financial commitment, reflecting the core principles of sacrifice and devotion. In the Quran, Hajj is beautifully depicted as a migration of hearts: *"Our Lord, I have settled some of my offspring in a valley without vegetation, near Your Sacred House. Our Lord, so that they may establish prayer. So make some people's HEARTS incline towards them"* (*Q* Ibraheem 37).

The pivotal switch that grants permission for this spiritual transformation is embodied in the **Black Stone**, a significant symbol during the Hajj. Throughout history, this switch has also been represented in human form by the prophets of each era and by God's Allies **(Awliyaa')**, who have guided believers in the periods following the passing of the Prophet Muhammad (PBUH). Through their example, seekers are invited to align their hearts with the divine, navigating the path of submission and connection to the Spirit.

Hajj symbolizes the migration of hearts towards unity, represented by the Kaaba's four-walled structure, which forms a cohesive heart. Thus, the Kaaba embodies the gateway to the **Spirit, centered** at its core.

Truth seekers must embark on a ritual journey that takes them from their physical selves to a heart-like internal space. This space can be understood as the gateway to a maze that leads to the truth of the Spirit embedded within this inner core. This internal space is not the muscular heart but a complex cavity seen as the entrance to truth, representing the Divine Spirit.

The Quran describes the heart as an entity that thinks, sees, and understands: *"We have created many of the jinn and men whose end shall be Hell! They have hearts, but they cannot understand"* (*Q* al-A'raf 180). It also questions, *"Have they not traveled on Earth so that they may have hearts to comprehend or ears to hear? It is not the eyes that go blind, but the hearts within the chests that do"* (*Q* al-Hajj 47).

As mentioned, these hearts can become locked: *"Will they not, then, ponder the Qur'an, or are there locks on their hearts?"* (*Q* Muhammad 25). Furthermore, these locks can rust with heedlessness: *"What they have earned has rusted their hearts"* (*Q* Mutaffifeen 15).

Therefore, this journey is about overcoming the idolized Self (Jihad-u-Nafs) to achieve unity with the pure, true Self (the Muhammadian Light). Along the way, seekers strive to conquer the treasure-box-shaped, four-chambered hearts (the Internal Kaaba) in search of the divine secret or Spirit within.

Throughout history, the concept of human intermediary (Wasita) authority as a permission holder has encountered resistance. As the Quran states, *"And nothing has prevented people from believing when guidance came to them, except that they said, 'Has Allah sent a man as a Messenger?"* (*Q* Israa 95). In another verse, it is noted, *"They replied, 'You are nothing but men like us, and the Gracious God has not revealed anything. You are only lying"* (*Q* Ya Sin 16). The lingering pride that humans have inherited from Satan often leads to resistance against accepting the necessary role of an intermediary link to the divine. Messengers', prophets', and the Awliyaa's most challenging task was to help people free themselves from this inherited Satanic pride aspect. The heavier the Satanic imprint, the greater the self-pride, and the stronger the denial from the messengers. This challenge has faced all of Prophet Muhammad's successors from his household, particularly the Allies of God (Awliya). The most vigorous resistance has often come from religious scholars who prefer to retain the honour they have acquired within the confines of temples.

Masculine and feminine creation:

In Arabic, the Quran refers to the Divine 'Spirit' as male and the Self as female, using pronouns.

Considering the Spirit as the highest unified attribute of Allah's singularity, we can view the Self as the highest multiplied and diverse manifestation of the unified Spirit of Allah in an intriguing cascade of manifestations of 'goodness.' This cascading manifestation descends further until it reaches the furthest point of Goodness, beyond which evil exists. The Adamic couple represented the dual attribute before eating from the tree. After they ate from the tree, they introduced another dimension to their capacity for falling into an evil trap called the lowest of the low. *"We have created man in the best make. Then We regressed him as the lowest of the low. Except for those who believed and did good works, so for them, is an uninterrupted reward"* (*Q* al-Tin 5-7).

As one moves further away from the primary dual presentation of the Divine Spirit and Self, the essence becomes denser and diminished in this devolution process. The Divine Spirit is defined by its unifying quality and acts as a source for the diverse and scattered manifestations of the Divine Self. This Spirit can be likened to a colourless light that transforms into multiple rainbows when it passes through a prism. The stunning beauty of the rainbow's colours reflects the Spirit's colourless nature.

In Adam's initial creation, a Spirit was blown into a mud vessel. The heat from the fire of Divine love transformed the mud into a mould from which black smoke was extracted. Thus, the production of black smoke occurred after Adam's preparation but before the blowing of the divine breath. From the black smoke, the evil spirits (Jinn) originated, *"The Jinn He created from the black smoke of fire."* (Q ar-Rahman 16)

This process of love creates a divine distinction of Spirit that manifests in an array of expressions, ultimately leading to a cascade of shapes and solids emerging from nothingness, encompassing the entire journey from A to Z.

The highest truth in this cascade is the concept of a unified spirit, manifested as a radiant Self and the power of love. The most fundamental expression of goodness that reflects this truth within the realm of parables is represented by Adam and Eve, who were created from Adam. They are bound together by love and the instinctual urge to reproduce in the physical realm (a'lam al-Mulk).

Sharia law is a comprehensive instructional manual designed to educate individuals about the original realities and the characteristics associated with each. It establishes a clear distinction between males and females, particularly regarding some more complex issues, such as permission for polygamous marriage and the roles assigned to human males (representing the Spirit) versus human females (representing the Self). Males are granted the role of provision, while females are typically seen as embodying, beautifying, and receiving the characteristics of males.

Although this perspective may seem unusual in the context of 21st-century Western civilization, it has been the norm for the past 30,000 to 40,000 years, dating back to Adam's appearance on Earth. During this time, humans have explored their original clay origins and sought to reconnect with their Spiritual and Self-realities by adhering to the guidance provided in Sharia law, which was tailored for their era.

What about Satan? Satan represents the lowest of the lows, existing beyond the cascade of goodness. This state is often likened to evil; the impurities are compared to the black smoke produced when transforming mud into clay through earthly fire. Satan embodies the impurities that all of Adam's descendants must continually cleanse to truly understand their diverse Selves and merge into the singular essence of their Spirits.

Satan can not change his nature.

The embodiment of the Divine Spirit. The intricate topic of Jesus Christ (PBUH) in Christianity and Islam:

Remphasizing that Allah's Spirit is a guiding attribute for truth seekers is crucial. When Jesus came and declared that he manifested the divine spirit, people misinterpreted this distinction after his departure. They viewed him as God rather than the representative of a collective divine attribute. The Quran clearly states that Jesus (PBUH) is a Divine Spirit: *"Verily, the Messiah, Jesus, son of Mary, was a Messenger of Allah, His word which He sent down to Mary, and a Spirit from Him"* (Q an-Nissa 172). Additionally, *"When Allah will say, 'O Jesus, son of Mary, remember My favour upon you and your mother; when I strengthened you with the Spirit of holiness"* (Q Al-Maida 111). Furthermore, *"We gave Jesus, son of Mary, clear proofs and strengthened him with the Spirit of holiness"* (Q al-Baqara 254).

Jesus laid the groundwork for the next phase of the ultimate revelation of the secrets of the Secret, as embodied in the Prophet Muhammad (PBUH/HF). *"And remember when Jesus, son of Mary, said, 'O children of Israel, surely I am Allah's Messenger to you, fulfilling that*

159

which is before me of the Torah, and giving glad tidings of a
Messenger who will come after me. His name will be Ahmad.' And
when he came to them with clear proofs, they said, 'This is clear
enchantment" (Q As-Suff 7)

The descent of the Divine Spirit and the Self has a final destination that should not be crossed. Adam and Eve symbolize the Spirit, representing the unity of origin, while the Self represents individual, repetitive identities. Beyond them lies Satan's manifestation. Therefore, we refer to humankind's Spirit (ar-Rouh) and self (Nafs) as delimited manifestations of the Divine's Self and Spirit.

Spiritual Navigation (Sulook)

The Sharia law has three or more goals: lower, more finite physical goals (alam al-Mulk), higher and more expansive spiritual goals (alam al-Malakoot) related to self-recognition, and the highest objectives of spiritual gnosis from the realm of invincibility (alam al-Jabaroot).

The smaller goals are the initial mandatory step to ascending into the three divinely designed educational curricula. After one of the victorious fights, the Prophet PBUH/HF quoted: "We returned from the small struggle to face the bigger struggle, which is the struggle of the self."

Similarly, this perspective can be applied to any ritual or act and consistently reflects on the higher and broader reality—the divine, educational, and gnostic destination of the Islamic pillars: ritualistic prayer, fasting, charity, and pilgrimage. Reflecting on this leads to a deeper understanding of the first pillar of Islam, which is the declaration that "there is no deity but Allah, and Muhammad is His messenger." Can Allah and the Prophet be WITNESSED? The answer is clear and straightforward, but I will leave that as food for thought.

Personalization of realities:

Allah embodied every reality to manifest in creaturely form as a general principle. He informed us about the hidden darkness and impurities that accompany us during the journey of self-struggle and created Satan as a transgenerational living being. Thus, it is fair to create an Adamic creature to represent the embodiment of His Mercy, whose role is to counteract the darkness of Satan using the Light of the Merciful.

In Islamic Sufism, this chain of torchbearers of light never ceases; it continues even after the passing of the Prophet Muhammad (PBUH) through selected people from the offspring of his daughter Fatima and her husband, Ali. Peace be upon them all.

Thus, we may refer to the prophets and messengers as the embodied or higher forms of prayer, fasting, pilgrimage, and purified charity of their time and community. The reader may accept the previous idea of the embodiment of reality in a good person from the past with skepticism. However, applying this concept to the present time poses a significant challenge for many people who adhere to double standards. This notion represents the pinnacle of God's friendship (Wilaya) concept, and anyone who comprehends this notion and seeks the individual who embodies this reality belongs to the elite few truth seekers.

Love is embodied by the helpful warmth of the earthly fire, beyond which harmful fire lies. Crossing the boundary of goodness or descending to the 'lowest of the low' depths occurs when one fails to adhere to the commands suggested by the Creator. In such cases, love morphs into fornication, earning turns into stealing, true emotions degrade into lust, and the fire of existence shifts from warmth and comfort into destructive burning. When Ibrahim (Abraham) was

161

amidst the fire, his Spirit—reflecting a gnostic understanding—returned to its original state of coolness and peacefulness, *"They said, 'Burn him and make you gods victorious, if at all you mean to do something. We said, 'O fire, be thou cold and a means of safety for Ibrahim"* (Q al_Anbiya 69-70).

On the other hand, the severe and lowest level of the fire of punishment on the Day of Judgment loses its initial cooling quality. Allah describes the fate of the transgressors in the afterlife, stating: *"They will taste neither coolness nor drink"* (Q al-Nabaa 25).

The Divine Book. The scrolls of Ibrahim and Moses, the Torah, the Injeel, and the Quran.

The opening of the book:

The Spirit is the messenger to the Self, but what message does it convey?

Allah is all-seeing and eternally satisfied with His goodness. As the all-knowing, the concept of satisfaction allows for a flow of understanding. Being singular (Ahad), Allah embodies all indivisible characteristics of goodness.

This singularity's manifestation requires the veils of oneness, meaning one entity can appear in various 'manifestations' (Tajilliat). For example, the same teacher may wear different attire to convey a topic to students. Similarly, we can view the One as a singular messenger conveying the essence of the One to many.

The multitude of The One resembles expressing the same idea with infinite rephrasing capabilities while preserving the core message, though cloaked in varying arrangements of letters.

Likewise, the Spirit (ar-Rouh) represents the message carrier of the divinely hidden secret of love, or as a subtle flow within a person's being, conveying the idea of personal satisfaction and pleasure when looking at oneself in the mirror.

The singularity is a secret; consequently, communicative speech is part of the hidden treasure. Therefore, to carry the original collective all-inclusive love message from the singularity as a flow of knowledge, the Spirit's attribute takes the love and satisfaction with 'goodness' to the Self's attributes to diverge as infinite representations of the same message.

The aforementioned is analogous to creating a personal legacy book, a moment of self-satisfaction and collective thought that transforms into a mental tool for self-recognition. This process leads to an overwhelming and highly energized sense of fulfillment that triggers a teardrop of joy. This teardrop embodies the essence of seeing, comprehending, and energizing the flow of knowledge. It is essential to acknowledge that all analogous parables remain valid when considering that the sequence of events is an illusory educational tool. The Divine's occurrence is simultaneous and eternal, and not sequential.

The Spirit conveys the message's teardrop-like essence to the Self to initiate the 'manifestation cascade' and transform the One into numerous individually distinguished Ones.

In the realm of examples, the physical (Mulk), spiritual (Malakoot), and invincible (Jabaroot) realms each convey the message of love in distinct ways. The process begins with a mysterious, wholesome, and exclusive speech in the Jabaroot called 'a Dot'. The Spirit's attribute transmits the Dot's essence to the Malakoot. The personalized spirit in the Malakoot is the archangel Jibreel, depicted differently, while the Self's infinite manifested realities are embodied as angels. In the physical realm (a'alam al-Mulk), the dots illustrate a cascading final destination as the Divine-scripted books, with the most definitive book being the latest revealed text, the Quran.

Thus, the process (sending down) of revelation for the Divine book began with a single Dot in Jabaroot, which was later expanded into a series of dots representing the first phrase of the book's opening (Basmalah). The 'Basmalah' further divides into the seven verses of the book's opening (al-Fatiha) and is considered the 'Mother of the book.' Subsequently, the further differentiation of the original Dot contributes to the composition of the Divine book.

Here are some supportive verses from the Quran: "He it is Who has sent down to you the Book; in it are verses that are decisive in meaning; they are the essence of the Book" (Q Al-Imran 8). Another verse states, *"Allah effaces and establishes, and He has the essence of the Book"* (*Q* Ar-Raad 40).

The Fatiha is also referred to as the "seven verses of dualities," *suggesting that it possesses a distinct collective identity different from the rest of the Quran: "We have indeed given you the seven from dualities and the Great Qur'an"* (*Q* Al-Hijr 88). This sevenfold nature of the Fatiha is reflected in the cosmos, which is structured around a seven-based system of creation that includes seven heavens, seven earths, and seventy veils, among others.

Thus, the Fatiha represents the reality of the seven heavens, the seven earths, prophethood, messengership, and divine companionship. The secret of the Fatiha lies in the primordial collective secret, symbolized by the Dot in the realm of Jabaroot. Quranic verses illustrate the stars in the sky and disciples on Earth: "My companions are like stars; with whomever you seek, you will find guidance" (Hadeeth).

The Heart

The concept of the in-between partition, known as Barzakh, is mentioned in the Quran. Surah ar-Rahman states, *"He has made the two bodies of water meet."* (*Q* ar-Rahman 20). In Surah al-Furqan, it further mentions, *"He caused the two seas to flow, one palatable and sweet, and the other saltish and bitter; between them, He has placed a barrier and a great partition."* (*Q* al-Furqan 54). Additionally, Barzakh refers to the state of the soul after death, serving as a barrier or partition between the physical world and the spiritual world. The Barzakh, which exists between the Spirit and the Self-dual, is called the 'Heart.' The Quran describes this entity as a mysterious, sovereign force that reflects a person's true essence.

The concept of cosmic structure can be visualized through the framework of seven heavens and seven layers of Earth, each representing a distinct unit corresponding to its celestial counterpart. The lowest layer of the sky is depicted as an upwardly convex arc, which connects with the upper, downwardly convex shape of the first layer of Earth. This configuration symbolizes the universe's heart, encompassing four horizontal directions—East, West, North, and South—and two vertical directions—up and down. At the center of this heart is the four-chambered cubical structure known as the Kaaba, which is both floored and roofed.

The physical heart is the innermost central organ of the human body. It comprises four chambers with upward and downward pumping capabilities. The heart receives deoxygenated blood from various tissues and pumps oxygenated blood, sustaining a critical relationship with the lungs. The interdependence of the heart and lungs is essential for optimal physiological functioning. This muscular organ operates autonomously, facilitating blood circulation throughout the body.

In the context of an individual's internal journey toward truth, the heart is an internal cavity that can lead the seeker upward toward Spirit unity or downward toward the Self's infinite diversities within the boundaries of front, back, left, or right. The leftward direction leads to sin and arrogance of the mind, the backward direction leads to ignorance, and the downward direction leads to the fire of desires and lusts. These directions are undesirable, leading to straying. Conversely, the other directions are desirable and resemble an ocean with three layers of darkness.

On the other hand, the upward direction leads to the heaven of gnosis, the rightward direction leads to mercy, and the forward direction leads to forgiveness — these are illuminated directions. The Quran mentions the people of the 'Right' and the people of the 'Left,' and that receiving one's book by the left hand or from a backward direction is a sign of certain doom:

"Whoever is given his book in his left hand will say: 'I wish I had not been given my record!'" (*Q* al-Haqqah 26).

"Whoever is given his book in his right hand will say: 'Come, read my book." (*Q* al-Haqqah 20).

"Him who will have his record given to him behind his back. He will call for destruction, and he will burn in a blazing Fire." (*Q* al-Inshiqaq 11-13).

In the Quran, Allah praises those who receive their book with their right hands — the illumination acquired by moving in the right direction or forward — and describes how they see this light manifesting in their right hand and before them. Hypocrites will be asked to relive the backward movement status they acquired in the first life:

"That day, you see the believing men and the believing women, their light running before them and on their right hands. 'Glad tidings for you today! Gardens underneath which streams flow, wherein you will abide.' That day, the hypocritical men and women will say to those who believe, 'Wait for us a while, so we may borrow some of your light.' It will be said to them, 'Go back and seek for light.' Then, a wall with a door will be set up between them. The inside of it will be all mercy, and outside of it, in front, will be torment." (Q al-Hadeed 13-14)

These three 'horizontal' directions, the undesired left and the desired right or forward function within the heart during the internal truth-seeking journey that is summed up in Surah al-Waqi'a:

"You shall be divided into three groups: The companions of the right hand — how lucky are those on the right hand! And the companions of the left hand — how unlucky are those on the left hand! And the foremost; they are truly the foremost. Those are the drawn near" (Q al-Waqi'a 8-12).

During the spiritual journey, the heart serves as a gateway, linking the divine manifestations of the Spirit and the Self. It operates similarly to a border control checkpoint, allowing passage only to those with the requisite credentials. Individuals who embody the quality of 'Goodness' can freely move through this heart barrier. In contrast, those facing challenges related to their heart, Self, or Spirit must first secure the necessary support for progression. The heart permits upward direction to the Spirit for those drawn near:

"Now if he is of those who are drawn near, then for him is a Spirit and fragrance of happiness and Garden of Bliss" (*Q* al-Waqi'a 89-90).

Correlation to the Realm of Letters:

The disclosure of the mysterious, hidden Divine treasure referred to as the *Treasure* Dot occurs using the parable of a train moving from upwards downwards and stopping at designated stations (Maqamat): The first is the Divine Singularity (maqam Ahadiya) station that remains undisclosed and non-comparative — the station of the Spirit and the station of the Self.

The singularity status is followed by the Oneness station (maqam Wahidiya). This station is manifested in the world of the physical realm (a'alam al-Mulk), showing the non-repetitive nature of anything, from human shapes, forms, and personalities to the unique appearance of every single snowflake. Consequently, the One is seen everywhere but with varying degrees of manifestation, referred to as scaling (Taqdeerat). The One manifests in both the Arabic and English languages as a straight line. In Arabic, this is represented by the letter 'Aleph', serving as the symbol of Oneness in the realm of Arabic letters.

All digits from one to nine are considered mere repetitions of the digit one, while Arabic letters are seen as curving repetitions of the letter Aleph (ﺍ). Consequently, the letter Aleph represents the digit one in the realm of letters. In Sufi science, this is portrayed as the numerological *Reference of Letters*. For example, the reference number for the letter 'Ba' is two.

The manifestation of the second station in the realm of letters is the curving of the Aleph's straight line to transition into another letter shape. A curved Aleph is called 'Lam' (ﻝ) in Arabic. The Lam

168

represents the Spirit that conveys the reality of the Aleph. The Lam is considered a disguised Aleph behind the veil of curvature. In the world of meaning, shape curving denotes leaning toward something and adding decorative design. As if the Lam shape itself says: "I am a disguised Aleph that longs to be known and appears in various manifestations." The Lam shape is still as infinite as the Aleph, with no visible beginning or end. Lam is the Spirit manifestation in the realm of letters; its number reference is 'seventy.' This multiple of seven reflects the seventy veils of the hidden treasure, the seven days of creation, the seven heavens, and the seven layers of Earth.

Finally, the Self (Nafs) is represented in the realm of letters as the Arabic letter 'Ha' (ه). Ha's shape is a closed circle, representing the limitation of the non-delimited characteristics of the Aleph and Lam. The "Ha" is like a screen or the disclosure theatre of the Divine Names and Attributes of 'The Most Goodness.' The "Ha" is delimited; therefore, it holds Sharia law and the dos and don'ts. Since the journey of humankind is a return from the delimited Self to the non-delimited Spirit and Aleph manifestations, the journey always begins by following the prescribed guidance. Sufi practitioners consider the "Ha" as the gate to divine knowledge.

May Allah strengthen our connection with our master Muhammad and his family, just as He did with our master Ibrahim and his family. May Allah bless our master Muhammad and his family, just as He has blessed our master Ibrahim and his family.

Glossary

1. **Allah**: The supreme and only deity in Islam, whose attributes, essence, and manifestations are explored through creation and revelation.

2. **Lordship (Rubūbiyya)**: A divine relational system representing the Creator's nurturing and sustaining role in relation to the creation.

3. **Servanthood**: The state of being a servant to Allah, characterized by worship, submission, and learning through divine guidance.

4. **Aḥadiyya (Oneness)**: The state of divine singularity, emphasizing Allah's uniqueness and indivisibility.

5. **Duality (Lordship/Servanthood)**: The relational aspect of Allah as the Lord and humankind as servants, reflecting a dynamic interaction.

6. **Thing-hood (Marḥalat al-shayʾiyya)**: The phase where humankind emerges as distinct entities composed of elements like clay, fire, water, and air.

7. **Primordial Light (Muḥammadian Light)**: The foundational divine light, central to creation and representing Allah's attributes.

8. **Sacred Phase**: A pre-material and holy stage in human existence characterized by divine praise, worship, and remembrance.

9. **Furqān**: The recognition of divine traces in the dispersed manifestations of creation.

10. **Pre-Atomic Phase**: A spiritual state preceding physical creation, described as a sea of light and divine knowledge.

11. **The Trust (Amanah)**: The responsibility given to humankind to act as stewards of Allah's creation and uphold divine principles.

12. **Embryonic Phase**: A metaphor for humanity's early state, likened to an embryo immersed in the divine amniotic fluid of praise and worship.

13. **Multiplicity (Shirk)**: The state of polytheism or associating partners with Allah, in contrast to divine unity.

14. **Satan (Iblis)**: The entity symbolizing ignorance, arrogance, and denial of divine authority.

15. **Day of Gathering**: The eschatological event where all beings are resurrected and held accountable for their deeds.

16. **Prostration of Angels**: The acknowledgment of Adam's divine knowledge and representation of Allah's names by the angels.

17. **Qabdah Muhammadiyah**: Muhammadiyan fist of light. A sample of the Divine light reflection depicts the great news of the divine unveiling.

18. **The Hidden Secret (Sirr)**: Allah's essence, which remains incomprehensible and transcendent to human understanding.

19. **Orbit (Hadd)**: The divine boundaries within which each creation operates.

20. **Heart (Qalb)**: The spiritual center of a human being, containing divine secrets and capable of ultimate divine perception.

21. **The Book (Kitab)**: The record of deeds presented on the Day of Judgment, encapsulating human actions.

22. **Non-Manifest Names (Batin Names)**: Divine qualities not revealed to humankind, representing hidden aspects of Allah's essence.

23. **Divine Essence (Dhat Allah)**: The core, incomprehensible being of Allah, beyond attributes and manifestations.

24. **Witnessing (Shahada)**: The act of testifying to Allah's Lordship and recognizing His sovereignty.

25. **Alaqa (Hanging Drop)** – A stage of pure spiritual growth, symbolizing the developmental phase of the self.

26. **Alam al-Malakoot (Spiritual Realm)** – The higher metaphysical dimension that the seeker journeys through for divine knowledge.

27. **Alam al-Mulk (Physical Realm)** – The material world is governed by rules and regulations, preparing individuals for higher spiritual understanding.

28. **Alam al-Jabaroot (Realm of Invincibility)** – The transcendent divine dimension beyond human comprehension.

29. **Bedaa (Heresy or Innovation)** – A term used to accuse illuminated individuals of deviating from traditional knowledge.

30. **Fana (Annihilation into Divine Essence)** – The ultimate phase of self-realization, where the seeker dissolves into divine awareness.

31. **Fasl (Disconnection)** – The state of lacking spiritual connection, often represented by people of wickedness.

32. **Jihad al-Nafs (Struggle Against the Self)** – The internal battle against desires and shortcomings.

33. **Sabeqoon (Forerunners)** – The highest-ranking spiritual seekers, leading the righteous path.

34. **Tajelliyat (Divine Disclosure)** – The unveiling of hidden divine realities.

35. **Unification (Tawheed)** – The ultimate realization that all manifestations stem from a singular divine reality.

www.ingramcontent.com/pod-product-compliance
Lightning Source LLC
Chambersburg PA
CBHW021635120626
46545CB00002B/561